SHAMBHALA DRAGON EDITIONS

The dragon is an age-old symbol of the highest spiritual essence, embodying wisdom, strength, and the divine power of transformation. In this spirit, Shambhala Dragon Editions offers a treasury of readings in the sacred knowledge of Asia. In presenting the works of authors both ancient and modern, we seek to make these teachings accessible to lovers of wisdom everywhere.

Self-Portrait by Hakuin

THE ESSENTIAL TEACHINGS OF ZEN MASTER HAKUIN

A translation of the
Sokkō-roku Kaien-fusetsu

by NORMAN WADDELL

SHAMBHALA
Boston & London
1994

Shambhala Publications, Inc.
Horticultural Hall
300 Massachusetts Avenue
Boston, Massachusetts 02115

9 8 7 6 5 4 3 2 1

First Edition
Printed in the United States of America on acid-free paper ⊗
Distributed in the United States by Random House, Inc., and in Canada by
Random House of Canada Ltd

Library of Congress Cataloging-in-Publication Data

Hakuin, 1686–1769.
   [Sokkōroku kaien fusetsu. English]
   The essential teachings of Zen Master Hakuin/translated by
Norman Waddell.
     p. cm.
   Includes bibliographical references and index.
   ISBN 0-87773-972-2
   1. Rinzai (Sect)—Doctrines—Early works to 1800. 2. Zen
Buddhism—Doctrines—Early works to 1800. I. Waddell, Norman.
II. Title.
BQ9399.E594S643413   1994   93-39948
294.3'42—dc20   CIP

Dedicated to my mother and father

ONE DAY IN MINO PROVINCE I observed a cicada casting its skin in the shade. It managed to get its head free, and then its hands and its feet emerged one after the other. Only its left wing remained inside, still caught to the old skin. It didn't look as though it would ever get that wing unstuck. Watching it struggling to free itself, I was moved by feelings of pity to assist it with my fingernail. Excellent, I thought, now you are free to go on your way. But the wing that I had touched remained shut and would not open. That cicada never was able to fly as it should have. Looking at it, I felt ashamed of myself and regretted deeply what I had done. When you think about it, present-day Zen teachers act in much the same way when they guide their students. I've seen and heard how they take young people of exceptional talent—those destined to become the very pillars and ridgepoles of our school—and with their extremely ill-advised and inopportune methods end up making them into something halfbaked and unachieved. This is a direct cause of the decline of our Zen school, the reason the Zen gardens are withering away.

—from a letter by Hakuin to Layman Kokan

CONTENTS

TRANSLATOR'S INTRODUCTION

Zen master Hakuin Ekaku, 1685–1768, the author of these talks, is the major figure of Japanese Rinzai Zen. During a long life spent as a country priest in a tiny rural temple, Hakuin almost singlehandedly reformed and revitalized a Zen school that, except for a brief interval in the previous century, had been in a state of spiritual lethargy for nearly three hundred years. In so doing, he laid the foundations for a method of Zen training that has enabled his school to continue as a spiritual force to the present day. When Hakuin died, he had redefined Zen for Japanese people in the modern era. In recent years, recognition of his achievements as a painter and calligrapher have gained him a reputation, beyond the sphere of religion, as one of the most versatile and original artists of the Edo period (1600–1868).

The Japanese title of the present work, *Sokkō-roku Kaien-fusetsu*, goes rather awkwardly into English as "Talks Given Introductory to Zen Lectures on the Records of Sokkō" (Sokkō, Hsi-keng in Chinese, was a sobriquet used by the Sung-dynasty Chinese priest Hsü-t'ang Chih-yü, 1185–1269, whose name in Japanese is Kidō Chigu). It is considered one of Hakuin's most important works and, in spite of its difficulty, one of the best introductions to his Zen teaching. Written in Chinese *Kambun*, that is, Chinese as read and written by the Japanese, it consists of a series of "general talks" or discourses (*fusetsu*) on Zen that Hakuin gave to students at the start of a large meeting he conducted at his home temple, Shōin-ji, in the spring of 1740. The formal Zen lectures or *teishō* at that meeting were devoted to *The Records of Sokkō*, a master Hakuin held in special veneration as an exemplar of the authentic Zen traditions to which he aspired. Normally, the purpose of giving informal talks of this kind at the beginning of a lecture meeting would be to encourage students in their practice in preparation for the training session and the more formal *teishō* to follow.

In fact, Hakuin took the occasion to deliver a full-length treatise on Zen. It incorporated virtually all his basic views on Zen teaching and training, and proclaimed his firm determination to rectify the erroneous views and practices into which he believed the school had strayed and which were directly responsible for its sharp decline. It called on the Zen community to return to the mainstream koan or *kanna* ("introspecting the koan") practice, which, through the efforts of masters like Hsü-t'ang, had flourished in China during the Sung dynasty and had formed the basis for the golden age of Japanese Zen in the thirteenth and fourteenth centuries.

Hakuin's effort was to convince students that the Zen being taught in contemporary temples was false, hence ineffective, and that freedom lay in the authentic realization attained through the way of *kenshō,* or enlightenment. He proceeded to demonstrate—using the examples of eminent Zen figures of the past as well as the experience he had gained during his own long religious struggle—that this freedom could not be attained by anything less than total dedication to a vigorous program of koan study directed toward, and later beyond, enlightenment.

The main themes of Hakuin's Zen teaching that appear over and over again in his later writings are here enunciated for the first time: the need to take the "poison" words or koans of the ancients and work into them with a single-minded determination and spirit of intense inquiry until the "Great Death," or breakthrough into enlightenment, is experienced; the necessity to deepen and mature the initial realization through continued practice beyond *kenshō*—so-called postenlightenment training; the need to produce some enlightened utterance of one's own to "trouble future generations of students"; and, finally, sharp denunciations of modern-day Zen teachers, whom he blamed for Zen's decline, especially those who included Pure Land practices in their training, or favored the doctrines of "silent meditation." It should be mentioned that while the term *silent meditation*, or *silent illumination*, is normally descriptive of the methods of the Sōtō sect, Hakuin uses it more generally as a condemnation of virtually all contemporary teachings.

Hakuin was fifty-two when he composed these talks, in the full flush of his powers. That his reputation had now spread far beyond the borders of his native Suruga province can be seen from the fact that four hundred students gathered from all parts of the country at the Shōin-ji Temple to take part in the great lecture meeting of 1740. It marked a turning point in his career; from that time on, for the remainder of his life, Hakuin dedicated himself with a fierce energy and determination to accomplishing his program of reforming the Zen school. It is a measure of his success that when he died Rinzai Zen was alive and well, flourishing with a strengthened vitality it hadn't seen for centuries.

The method of Zen training that Hakuin developed over the second half of his career was carried on and systematized by an unusually large contingent of talented followers. The names of fifty of those who received his sanction are known, but it is said that there were probably at least twice that many. Today, virtually all Rinzai masters trace their descent from him. The Rinzai school is now, practically speaking, the school of Hakuin.

THE SOURCES OF HAKUIN'S ZEN

The first Zen temple was established in Japan in the early decades of the thirteenth century. In the next one hundred and seventy-five years, over a score of Zen teaching lines were brought to Japan and established there, either by Chinese priests who came from the continent, or by Japanese monks who had studied in China and received sanction from Chinese teachers. From Hakuin's standpoint, the most important of those transmissions was the one introduced by a Japanese disciple of Hsü-t'ang Chih-yü named Nampo Jōmyō, 1235–1309, better known by his posthumous title Daiō Kokushi.

Nampo traveled to China in 1259 at the age of twenty-four. After studying with Hsü-t'ang for a number of years, some of them spent as his attendant, Nampo attained enlightenment and received Hsü-t'ang's certification. When Nampo was about to return to Japan, Hsü-t'ang wrote a farewell verse in his honor. It concluded with the line, "My descendants will increase daily beyond the Eastern Seas." This became known in later Japanese Zen as "Kidō's prophecy."

Daiō returned to Japan in 1267 and taught for more than forty years at temples in Kyūshū, Kyoto, and Kamakura. He had many able disciples, including one student of great distinction, Shūhō Myō-chō (1282–1338)—known by his honorary title Daitō Kokushi. Daitō is credited with having achieved a depth of attainment exceeding that of Daiō himself. Daitō went on to become founder of the Daitoku-ji Temple in Kyoto and produced two main heirs, Tettō Gikō (1295–1369), who succeeded him at Daitoku-ji, and Kanzan Egen (1277–1360), who later founded the Myōshin-ji Temple, also in Kyoto. A handful of celebrated priests, among them Ikkyū Sōjun (1394–1481) and Takuan Sōhō (1573–1645), appeared in the first centuries of Daitoku-ji's history, but by the 1600s the influence of the Daitoku-ji teaching line was in decline, overshadowed by those of the other large Kyoto monasteries. It was at this time that the Myōshin-ji branch, the one to which Hakuin traced his descent, began its rise to prominence. Myōshin-ji priests, teaching for the most part, like Hakuin, in smaller temples located in the provinces, dominated Rinzai Zen throughout the Edo period.

To Hakuin, the authentic Zen tradition was powerfully represented in the lineage of four priests: Hsü-t'ang, Daiō, Daitō, and Kanzan. These men were figures of pivotal importance. They had brought to Japan and firmly established there the only surviving teaching line that transmitted the orthodox Zen of the great Chinese masters. Soon after Hsü-t'ang's death, the original teaching of this line had begun a rapid (catastrophic, Hakuin would say) decline in China, corrupted by the increasing introduction of Pure Land Buddhist practices into Zen training.

By receiving the transmission from Hsü-t'ang and taking it to Japan, Daiō had, in effect, saved it from extinction. Hakuin wrote of Daiō's unique achievement in a marginal note he inscribed in a copy of Daiō's Zen records:

> Daiō was the only priest who attained the true, untransmittable essence that had been handed down from the great masters of the T'ang. He was the Japanese Bodhidharma. The reason Bodhidharma, among many other Zen patriarchs, is revered by all branches of Chinese Zen is because he was the one who brought the buddha-mind school [Zen] to China from India. Because Daiō went to China and returned having received the direct transmission of the Zen Dharma from Master Hsü-t'ang . . . he is the most

eminent by far of the twenty-four teachers who introduced Zen into Japan. For that reason, from the time I was a young priest, whenever I made an offering of incense, I never failed to offer some of it in honor of Daiō.

According to Hakuin's reading of Zen history, Daiō's Zen sustained its original vigor roughly until the fifteenth century. It then fell sharply as literature and scholarship began to take the place of actual religious practice. It managed somehow to remain alive—"a thin, fragile thread"—until the seventeenth century, when a great abbot of Myōshin-ji named Gudō Tōshoku (1579–1661) appeared and gave it new life. It was through a "Dharma grandson" of Gudō named Shōju Rōjin (1642–1721) that Hakuin received the transmission. The teachings of this somewhat shadowy master, which exist only in the extensive passages that Hakuin presents in his own writings, are filled with Shōju's deep concern over the sorry state of contemporary Zen. "True teachers," he said, "were harder to find than stars in a midday sky." He told Hakuin that unless he produced an heir who could carry on the orthodox transmission, it would "fall into the dust" and die out forever.

Standing in his way was the Zen establishment of the time, "heterodox" priests who had "infested the land, planted themselves in positions of power, and shamelessly and willfully turned their backs on Zen tradition." Hakuin had seen more than enough of these men in his travels as a young monk. He speaks of three general types among his contemporary teachers: "do-nothing" Zennists, "silent meditation" Zennists, and *nembutsu* Zennists. These three labels are normally applied to adherents of the Rinzai, Sōtō, and Ōbaku sects, respectively, but often Hakuin makes no attempt to differentiate between them; in his eyes, they are all equally guilty of debilitating Zen by espousing passive and quietistic approaches to practice.

By instructing their pupils to do nothing but sit in silent meditation, to combine practices such as the recitation of the Buddha's name (*nembutsu*) with Zen, or by curtailing or eliminating the use of the koan in Zen training, such teachers had deprived students of the very thing Hakuin believed was vital to the success of their efforts: a "great, driving spirit of inquiry that cannot rest until satori is achieved." While he might admit the suitability of *nembutsu* recitation for students of inferior or even mediocre ability, for students of Zen, who belong to the "highest class of the highest rank" of Buddhist disciple, the adoption of such methods was nothing less than an admission of spiritual defeat. "If that happens," he said,

> we will see all the redoubtable members of the younger generation—people gifted with outstanding talent, who have it in them to become great Dharma pillars worthy to stand shoulder to shoulder with the celebrated Zen figures of the past—traipsing along after half-dead old duffers, sitting in the shade with listless old grannies, dropping their heads and closing their eyes and intoning endless choruses of *nembutsu*. . . . Whose children will be found to carry on the vital pulse of buddha-wisdom? Who will become the cool, refreshing shade trees to provide refuge for people in the latter day? All the authentic customs and traditions of the Zen school will disappear. The seeds of buddhahood will wither, turn hard and dry.

HAKUIN'S LIFE

Hakuin was born and spent his entire life, except for the years he was wandering the country on his Zen pilgrimage, in the tiny farming village of Hara, situated on the Tōkaidō Road near the foot of Mount Fuji. He was by all accounts inclined strongly toward religion at a very early age. At fifteen (by Japanese count) he entered religious life at the neighborhood Zen temple, Shōin-ji. The head priest, Tanrei, who performed the tonsure, was a family friend. He gave the young novice the religious name Ekaku, which he would use until his thirties when, upon being established as abbot of Shōin-ji himself, he adopted the additional name Hakuin. Four years later his teacher permitted him to set out on a pilgrimage to study with other Zen teachers around the country. His wanderings lasted fourteen years, taking him throughout most areas of the main island of Honshū and across to the island of Shikoku, to masters of all three Zen sects.

After the years of travel, seeking advice and instruction from many Zen teachers but mostly practicing on his own, at the age of thirty-one he sequestered himself in a remote hermitage in the mountains of Mino province, determined to make an all-out effort to attain a final breakthrough. While he was there, news reached him that his father had fallen critically ill and wanted him to return and reside in Shōin-ji, which was now vacant and in need of a priest. Hakuin, somewhat reluctant, agreed. His years of pilgrimage were now at an end.

The temple Hakuin had inherited was not only small and insignificant—"a branch temple of a branch temple"—it was also penniless, its buildings neglected and in an advanced stage of decay. The *Hakuin Nempu*, a religious biography of Hakuin compiled by his disciple Tōrei, gives some idea of what it was like at the time:

> Shōin-ji had fallen into an almost indescribable state of ruin. Stars shone through the roofs at night. The floors were constantly saturated by rain and dew. It was necessary for the master to wear a straw raincoat as he moved about the temple attending to his duties. He needed sandals inside the main hall when he went there to conduct ceremonies. Temple assets had passed into the hands of creditors, the temple equipment had all been pawned. . . . About the only thing worth noting around here," he said, "is the moonlight and the sound of the wind."

Shōin-ji remained Hakuin's home and the center of his teaching activity until his death fifty years later. A passage in Tōrei's biography describes Hakuin's life during the first ten years of his residency:

> He applied himself single-mindedly to his practice. He endured great privation without ever deviating from his spare, simple way of life. He didn't adhere to any fixed schedule for sutra-chanting or other temple rituals. When darkness fell he would climb inside a derelict old palanquin and seat himself on a cushion he placed on the floorboard. One of the young boys studying at the temple would come, wrap the master's body in a futon, and cinch him up tightly into this position with ropes. There he would remain motionless, like a painting of Bodhidharma, until the following day when the boy would come to untie him so that he could relieve his bowels and take some food. The same routine was repeated nightly.

Hakuin had achieved his initial entrance into enlightenment at twenty-four, during his pilgrimage. In the years that followed, he had other satori experiences, "large ones and small ones, in numbers beyond count." They had deepened and broadened his original enlightenment, but he still did not feel free. He was unable to integrate his realization into his ordinary life, and felt restricted when he attempted to express his understanding to others. The final decisive enlightenment that brought his long religious quest to an end occurred on a spring night in 1726, his forty-first year.

He was reading *The Lotus Sutra* at the time. It was the chapter on parables, where the Buddha cautions his disciple Shariputra against savoring the joys of personal enlightenment, and reveals to him the truth of the Bodhisattva's mission, which is to continue practice beyond enlightenment, teaching and helping others until all beings have attained salvation. Hakuin narrates the crucial moment in his autobiography, *Wild Ivy*:

> A cricket made a series of churrs at the foundation stones of the temple. The instant they reached the master's ears, he was one with enlightenment. Doubts and uncertainties that had burdened him from the beginning of his religious quest suddenly dissolved and ceased to exist. From that moment on he lived in a state of great emancipation. The enlightening activities of the buddhas and patriarchs, the Dharma eye to grasp the sutras—they were now his, without any doubt, without any lack whatever.

In Tōrei's biography, this experience is emphasized as the pivotal event in Hakuin's religious life. To this point, Hakuin's practice had been directed toward seeking his own enlightenment; from then on it was directed toward helping others achieve liberation. In doing this he would use to the full the extraordinary ability he had now acquired to "preach with the effortless freedom of the buddhas."

During his late thirties and forties, Hakuin accepted a small but growing number of students. His reputation slowly grew and spread until by his early fifties, when he composed these "Introductory Talks," his name was known and respected even in the halls of the great Myōshin-ji in Kyoto. The lecture meeting of 1740, according to Tōrei, established Hakuin as the foremost Zen teacher in the land.

Monks and nuns and lay people from all over the country began to converge on Shōin-ji. They came from all classes of society and all walks of life. Shōin-ji barely supplied its own needs; it was unable to accommodate even a small number of students, let alone the hundreds who were coming to receive instruction. Most of those who came were obliged to find lodging elsewhere.

They slept and practiced in private houses and abandoned dwellings, unused temples and halls, ruined shrines, under the eaves of farmhouses; some even camped out under the stars. The whole countryside for miles around the temple was transformed into a great center for Zen practice. It was a new kind of Buddhist assembly, formed and maintained by the monks themselves.

The records speak of the great awe in which Hakuin was held by his students. Tōrei remembered him as "a sheer cliff towering abruptly before him. A menacing presence stalking the temple like a great ox, glaring around with the eyes of an angry tiger." Something of the terror Hakuin must have struck into the hearts of students can be felt by standing before the effigy sculpture of Hakuin enshrined in the Founder's Hall at Shōin-ji. Even today it glares formidably out at the spectator.

The only students who remained were those who had come to study with the same deep motivation that had driven Hakuin. In a preface to Hakuin's *Idle Talks on a Night Boat*—signed by an anonymous student called "Hunger-and-Cold, the Master of Poverty Hermitage," who is obviously Hakuin himself—is a famous passage that draws a vivid picture of life at Shōin-ji:

> From the moment monks set foot inside Shōin-ji's gates they gladly endured the poisonous slobber the master spewed at them. They welcomed the stinging blows from his stick. Students stayed for ten, even twenty years, the thought of leaving never entering their minds. Some had resolved to lay down their lives there, and become dust under the temple pine trees. They were the finest flowers of the Zen groves, dauntless heroes to all the world. . . . They faced hunger in the morning, freezing cold by night. Sustaining themselves on wheat chaff and raw vegetables, they heard nothing but the master's blistering shouts and abuse, felt nothing but bone-piercing blows from his furious fist and stick. They saw sights that made their foreheads furrow; they heard things that made their bodies pour with sweat. There were scenes that would have brought tears to a demon's eyes, and would have caused a devil to

press his palms together in supplication. When these monks first arrived, they were in radiant health, with glowing skins, but before long their bodies were thin and emaciated, their faces drawn. . . . None of them could have been held a moment longer, were they not totally dedicated to their quest, begrudging neither health nor life itself.

But Hakuin was not always the flint-eyed teacher striking terror into the hearts of Zen students. He was also a man of great warmth and kindness and humor who shared the life of his fellow villagers and was deeply sympathetic to their needs. When he was not engaged in training his regular students, he was trying to reach out through writing and painting to educate the farmers, fishermen, and others of his native region and bring them closer to the truth of the Buddhist teaching.

Hakuin's biographical records show that the pace of his teaching activity actually picked up over the final twenty-five years of his life. He lectured regularly at Shōin-ji and other temples in the area on a wide range of Buddhist sutras and Zen texts. Invitations came from other temples and lay groups around the country asking him to conduct meetings. He willingly made journeys of days, even weeks, in order to respond to them. In addition, from his sixties on he turned more and more to writing, painting, and calligraphy to communicate his message, producing works in an unusually broad range of genres and themes.

It was not uncommon for Zen priests to engage in artistic pastimes. They were expected to be proficient calligraphers. But in Hakuin's case, these skills assumed a much greater importance. They became a central part of his teaching and one of the chief hallmarks of Hakuin Zen.

He left over fifty written works, ranging from difficult Zen discourses and specialized commentaries in Chinese designed for Zen students all the way to simple songs, recitations, and chants, in which he couched his Zen message in a highly colloquial language to make it accessible to the common people. Another characteristic seen throughout his work is his frequent and detailed reference to the circumstances of his own religious enlightenment. He uses accounts of his life in the same way that he does the stories of the Zen teachers of the past: to encourage students in their practice by telling them of the difficulties that others had experienced, and overcome, in the course of their Zen training.

He excelled in both painting and calligraphy, producing works in numbers that must have reached into the thousands. They too were his talks and his sermons, with an even more direct and universal appeal. His paintings include many traditional Zen subjects such as Bodhidharma, Shakyamuni, and other figures from Zen history. But he also invented new themes inspired by folk belief, village tales, and his own fertile imagination. His great versatility and inventiveness are evident in his calligraphy as well. Though he worked in a wide variety of styles, his bold compositions, filled with the thick, massive strength of his large-size characters, possess an ability unique even among Zen artists to translate visceral Zen experience to paper. Standing before them, the viewer is struck by a primordial power uncanny in its depths.

The late Yamada Mumon Roshi, who served as abbot of Myōshin-ji Temple, once wrote, "There was a saying in Hakuin's home province of Suruga, 'Suruga province has two things of surpassing greatness, Mount Fuji and Priest Hakuin.' I believe that in the not too distant future that saying will be changed to, 'Japan has two things of surpassing greatness, Mount Fuji and Priest Hakuin.'"

A number of annotated editions of Hakuin's Japanese writings have appeared over the past twenty years, yet until very recently little has been done to make his important Chinese writings such as *Sokkō-roku Kaien-fusetsu* and *Kaian-kokugo* more accessible. I must therefore express my gratitude to Gishin Tokiwa, whose modern Japanese translation of *Sokkō-roku Kaien-fusetsu* (*Hakuin*, Daijō butten 27, Chūokōron-sha, Tokyo, 1988) appeared as I was struggling to finish my English translation of the text. Professor Tokiwa's work has made my task far easier and simpler than it would otherwise have been. It was also through his help that I was able to procure a photocopy of a first edition of *Kaien-fusetsu* from the rare book collection of the Hanazono College library. It is inscribed throughout with glosses and notations in Hakuin's own hand and has been valuable in helping determine Hakuin's meaning.

I would like to thank Mr. Daisaburō Tanaka of Tokyo for generously allowing me to reproduce works from his fine collection of Hakuin's paintings and calligraphy; to Ryūtaku-ji Temple of Mishima, Ryūkoku-ji Temple of Akashi, and the Hisamatsu family of Gifu for reproducing works in their possession.

The Essential Teachings of Zen Master Hakuin

FOREWORD BY GENSHOKU

Explaining the circumstances that led to the
printing of the *Sokkō-roku Kaien-fusetsu*

In the twelfth month of the third year of Kampō
(1743), after the evening meal at the conclusion of the *Rōhatsu sesshin*
[the intensive meditation period beginning on the 8th day of the 12th
month], I [Genshoku] had a visitor who said:

I understand that Hakuin's Dharma talks are soon to be published
for students of Zen. In some quarters people are saying that his real
reason for publishing them is to establish his reputation as a Zen
teacher. They are jealous of him, and their criticism of him is so
intense they will do him real harm. But surely they are wrong. The
real reason these Dharma teachings are being published must lie elsewhere. As his attendant, don't you feel that you should speak out and
save your teacher from being hurt by these allegations?

I replied to him: Ah! I know what's being said. Some people like
nothing better than to spend their time disparaging others. But when
they direct their insinuations at someone like my master, they miss
the mark completely. If he had been motivated by such unseemly
aims, do you suppose for a moment eighty outstanding monks, the
mainstays of tomorrow's Zen school, would be camped in huts
around his temple? Shunning the mundane world completely because of their deep veneration for him? Why would they stay there,

undergoing all those hardships? It was perfectly clear to me from the moment I first met the master that he had absolutely no interest at all in making a reputation for himself. But inasmuch as you have requested it, I will for your sake explain how the publication of this work came about.

In spring of the fifth year of Gembun (1740), the master yielded to persistent urgings from students far and wide and delivered a series of lectures on *The Records of Sokkō*. He beat out a tune that instilled fresh life into Sokkō's [Hsi-keng's] ancient melodies.

Preparations for the lectures were set in motion the previous winter. After the meal at the anniversary of Bodhidharma's death, on the fifth of the tenth month, the score or so of ragged monks who lived in huts around Shōin-ji held a consultation and decided to get the temple ready for a lecture meeting. They worked together to make necessary repairs to Shōin-ji so it could accommodate a group of visiting students.

They shored up rickety old buildings. They reopened the shaft in the old well. They mended doors and windows. They strapped up broken roof beams. While brothers Taku, Tetsu, Sha, and Sū worked enthusiastically at these difficult tasks, Brother Kyū went searching far and wide to collect a store of grain and beans, and Brother Chū made the rounds of neighboring villages begging vegetables. The rest, working in shifts, labored feverishly through the days and long into the nights.

The master kept his distance while this was going on. Taking his attendants Jun and Kō, he slipped off and sought refuge at the Genryū-ji Temple in Kashima. He stayed there about ten days, then moved on to the Myōzen-ji Temple in Fujisawa. Finally, he went to Yoshimizu in Suruga, where he stayed with Ishii Gentaku, a layman living in seclusion there. He remained with Gentaku almost a whole month. All the time he was there, except when called upon to receive visitors, he devoted to sessions of deep and blissful sleep. His snores reverberated through the house like rumblings of thunder. They shook the foundations. They sent dust storms gusting through the rafters. He slept face to the floor, lying curled up like some great, well-fed snake. Visitors gazed on him in wonder.

Attendants Jun and Kō were greatly distressed. They pleaded with him: "Brother Chū has entrusted us with a grave responsibility. We must see that you dictate some Dharma talks that can be used to encourage the younger monks in their practice. We are supposed to write them down and take them back to the temple so they can be read to the brotherhood. It will offer them some relief from the work they've been doing."

The master nodded, a faint smile crossing his lips. But then he just turned over and resumed his snoring. Jun and Kō came again and again, like little children begging their parents to make good on a promise, pleading with him to forgo his slumber and begin dictating the talks.

Finally, he sat up. Shutting his eyes, he calmly and quietly started to speak. First five lines of transcript, then ten lines. He uttered them just as they came to his mind. After Kō took them down, Jun revised them. The master dictated sentence after sentence, with little concern for sequence or order. Kō's brush traced them tirelessly down on the paper. Master and disciples labored as one, completely engrossed in the work at hand. By the time they left Layman Gentaku's hermitage, fifty sheets of paper had been filled with writing.

Layman Gentaku remarked that "the three finest examples of Zen writing are reputed to be *Wan-an's Words of Instruction, Ta-hui's Letters*, and the *Dharma Teaching of Fo-yen*. But what Zen teacher until now, including Wan-an and Ta-hui, ever conjured up such an endless tangle of vines and branches as you have here?"

Then both he and the master clapped their hands and laughed loudly.

The master returned to Shōin-ji in the eleventh month. It was the day before the winter solstice. He invited us monks in for tea to show his appreciation for the work we had been doing. We were sitting in a circle around him, enjoying ourselves talking and sipping tea. Jun and Kō, seated side by side, brought out the master's Dharma talks and began to read them to us in the lamplight. We received them with open hearts, so jubilant we felt like dancing around the room. Our elation was soon forgotten as we became absorbed in the reading, which went on for several nights.

At the end of the assembly, when the master finished his lectures on *The Records of Sokkō*, the crowds of people who had taken part in the meeting gathered around him making their bows to him. We took the opportunity to ask him to allow the text of his Dharma talks to be published as a book.

Immediately, he called out in a loud voice for someone to bring him fire. We were greatly concerned for the safety of the manuscript, but Jun and Kō had the presence of mind to roll it up quickly and hide it in one of their robes. We brought the matter up again several times after that, when the chance presented itself. But now he just ignored us completely. Since then, three years have passed.

In autumn of this year senior monks Chū and Yaku visited the master in his quarters and said:

> If your Dharma talks are published, two things may happen to displease you. But if they are not published, it will have an undesirable effect on students engaged in Zen practice. To a person who is immersed in the practice of Zen, the Way is a vital living thing. He would not focus merely on the words when he read the work. To a person who is reading it as literature, constantly on the lookout for misused words or mistaken characters, the Way is neither vital nor alive. Such a person would no doubt be able to discover the kind of mistakes he is seeking. That is one of the things that may displease you.
>
> A wise man once wrote that when a tree grows so high that it towers above the other trees in the forest, it is certain to be buffeted by winds. And when a person does something that sets him above other people, it is inevitable that he will become the object of resentment. If your Dharma words are printed, it will be clear to all that you stand head and shoulders above your fellow priests. There are certain to be some who will criticize you for allowing it to be published. Some, vexed with envy, will gnash their teeth and try to cause trouble for you. That is the second of the things that may displease you.
>
> But even if it is not published, it is sure to be read nonetheless. In future, students will be vying to get their hands on a manuscript of it so they can make copies for themselves. They would continue to do that no matter what measures were taken to stop it. In the end, they would waste valuable time and energy, which should be spent on their practice, wielding their brushes. That is why I said that not publishing it would be harmful to students engaged in practicing the Way.

As for the first two concerns, they could be dealt with merely by resolving to endure the criticism. But if the work is not published, a large number of students will copy it anyway, wasting their valuable time and energy. Published, it may well draw censure from the learned. "It shouldn't have been published," they will declare. "You shouldn't have given the talks in the first place!" As your students, it would distress us greatly. But it is nonetheless true that there are many ways of helping Zen students and rendering service to the Dharma. Zen master Ta-hui did it when he burned the printing blocks of *The Blue Cliff Record*. And you would do it by having your Dharma words published. Who can say which act would have the greater merit?

After the master had heard us out, he said:

I'm well aware of all that you have said. But those "Dharma words" you keep referring to are just a lot of foolish twaddle. I spoke them without thinking, on the spur of the moment. I was still half asleep. It contains lapses of memory. Slips of the tongue. I can't allow something like that to be printed. People would just laugh at it. Maybe I can comply with your request later, after some wise and learned scholar has looked it over and corrected it.

These words gave us great encouragement. Brother Tōko set to work making yet another fair copy. Chō and Yaku began secretly checking the text for errors. When they had finished, Brother Chū put it into his sleeve and traveled to Tōtōmi province to visit Mr. Ono. Mr. Ono was delighted when Chū told him of our project and offered us his full support.

Chū went next to the Keirin-ji Temple in eastern Mino to see the priest Jōshitsu. After bowing reverently to Jōshitsu, Chū informed him of our plans. Then he earnestly requested him to write a preface for the work and check the manuscript for errors. Jōshitsu declined with great firmness. Chū persisted. Jōshitsu refused three more times, but finally, on the fourth request, he agreed. Chū came away feeling like someone who had obtained the priceless jewel that lies under the jaws of the black dragon.

From Mino, Chū continued on to the capital at Kyoto. On the way, by a miraculous stroke of luck, he happened to run into Kinokuniya Tōbei, a bookseller from the Numazu post-station near Shōin-ji. When Kinokuniya heard about the plan to print the master's words, he applauded our undertaking wholeheartedly, and pledged to use all the resources at his disposal to help further it. With his kind help, it was not long before the carving of the blocks and printing of the Dharma talks was carried through to completion.

Chū then sent a letter from Kyoto telling us all to "offer incense, face in the direction of eastern Mino, and press your palms together in supplication."

Ah! without Mr. Kinokuniya, Brother Chū never could have achieved such brilliant success, even if he had gone back and forth to Kyoto hundreds or even thousands of times. And had Kinokuniya not encountered Chū when he did and gone idly on to pursue worldly pleasures in the capital, the merit he achieved—linking him directly to buddhahood—would never have been possible. What is more, even had the two of them striven together in all sincerity, unless the manuscript had passed under the penetrating scrutiny of a wise teacher like Jōshitsu, it would not have been in any shape for Chū to take to Kyoto. In fact, it can be said that the present work could only have come about through the combination of all four elements—Chū, Kinokuniya, Jōshitsu's preface, and his revision.

Back at Shōin-ji, we informed the master of the events taking place far away in the capital. He was aghast. For several days he seemed to be in a state of shock. Then he told us he wanted someone to leave immediately for Kyoto to have the printing stopped. After consulting among ourselves, we went to him and said, "It would take days to reach Kyoto, and even when we got there, it is a great metropolis— there are said to be over a hundred thousand houses. How could we possibly find Chū and deliver your message?"

"How regrettable!" sighed the master mournfully. "A fool mistake I made several years ago when we were staying at Layman Gentaku's house. I just wanted to put a stop to Kō's whining. Now here I am biting my navel. Ahh! It is those Dharma talks of mine that will make men know me, and those same Dharma talks that will make them condemn me."

This is an outline of what I, Genshoku, saw and heard as I served at the master's side.

My visitor said, "The work isn't even published yet, and already criticism is widespread. Don't you think you should do what you can to diminish it by writing down what you have just told me and publishing it?"

I replied, "As the master's attendant, I have a duty to protect him, regardless of what happens to me. There is no reason to refuse to do what you suggest."

Hence I have written this down. My sole purpose is to answer those who would criticize my teacher.

Attendant Genshoku made an offering of incense and composed this foreword after the meal at services commemorating the Buddha's attainment of enlightenment. The third year of Kampō (1743).

1

LICKING UP HSI-KENG'S FOX SLOBBER

Long ago, at the beginning of the Chien-yen era (1127–1131) of the Southern Sung dynasty, the Zen priest Yüan-wu K'o-ch'in, residing at the Ling-ch'üan-yüan Temple on Mount Chia in Li-chou, delivered a series of lectures in which he commented on the hundred cases of Hsüeh-tou Ch'ung-hsien.[1] His fellow priest Ta-p'ing sent him a letter of reproach, using a tone of language harsher than one would expect from one's own flesh and blood.[2] But Yüan-wu realized the justness of the criticism and ceased from writing such commentaries. This ought to be a valuable lesson for us all.

So why am I about to commence licking up all the fox slobber that Priest Hsi-keng spewed and left behind him in those ten temples where he served?[3] Why am I about to brazenly ascend the high teaching seat, clutching a *hossu* [whisk] in my hand, to diminish the dignity of a whole hall full of senior priests?:

I was blown by the winds of karma to this broken-down old temple at the beginning of the Kyōhō era (1716–1736). I have remained here, without disciples, for the past twenty years. In that time, I have been visited by students from all corners of the land, asking me to give them talks and lectures on sutras and Zen writings. Some of them brought me rosters bearing names of hundreds of students. Others submitted their requests in elaborate compositions that were twenty or thirty lines long! All together, this must have happened at least thirty times. I can't tell you how it has interfered with my sleep!

A few of the students burned with genuine zeal and determination. They made the rounds of Zen teachers, asking them to intercede with me on their behalf. They went to lay followers, complaining of my intransigence. I saw how strongly they were committed to achieving their goal; I wanted to do what I could to respond to their needs. But my temple is extremely poor. The kitchen shelves are bare. From the far north of the country to the far south, I don't suppose a single soul could be unaware of the poverty here at Shōin-ji.

At the same time, I am deeply concerned about the sharp decline in Buddhist practice in recent years, and the sad decay of the Dharma. The young generation of monks are a pack of misfits—irresponsible and ungovernable rascals. When they first come to me, I cannot help loving them for their quiet, unassuming manner. My head bows before their sincere devotion and firm resolve. I think: "They are genuine monks determined to break through to enlightenment. Their thoughts are fixed firmly on the great matter of birth and death."

But before even a month is up, they turn from the exemplary norms and customs of the past as they would from dirt. The time-honored temple regulations mean no more to them than lumps of dry mud. They band together in groups and run roughshod through the temple, roaming the garden and corridors shouting out to one another in loud voices, loitering in passageways singing and humming. They pay no attention to what their superiors tell them. Senior priests and temple masters are powerless to restrain them.

They cut the bucket rope at the wall. They lift the temple bell from its moorings and turn it upside down. They push over the big temple drum. Whenever they get the chance, they sneak out the front gate. They slink furtively back in at night through openings they have burrowed in the temple wall. They gather in front of the main hall, capering about and singing shameless tunes they pick up in town. They swarm over the hill in back of the temple like ants, disturbing others with their wild clapping and horsing around. They prop sharp sickles up in dark corridors where the unsuspecting will walk into them, stack big water jars in passageways where people will be sure to knock them over. They crack the floor-planks over

the privy so that when men squat on them they will tumble into the
pit-filth. They plague the kitchen monks by dousing the firewood
with water so it can't be used to light the ovens in the morning.
They make the rounds of the local teahouses and wineshops, gleefully
abandoning themselves to base amusements.

While there could be a thousand people inside the temple devoting
themselves to their training with untiring zeal, because they do not
venture outside the gates for the entire retreat, no one knows of their
illustrious achievements. The rowdy miscreants haunting the town
streets engrossed in these unsavory pastimes may be no more than
two or three in number, but since it all takes place in broad daylight
for everyone to see, their black sins become known to all.

Ahh! because of the mindless and irresponsible actions of a handful of monks, tens of thousands of their fellows must share their noto-
riety. Jades are cast into the furnace along with ordinary stones. Gold
and steel are melted into one common lump. Buddhist monks have
come to be despised by good laymen and -women. Now they are as
welcome as a shit-covered pig or a mangy dog with running sores.
People in the streets condemn them. Even the masterless samurai talk
of their flagrant misdeeds.

It is deplorable, the harm they do. In one moment, the dignity and
authority of the Buddha's Way is lost, the radiance of the Dharma
teaching snuffed out. A troup of Yaksha demons eight thousand
strong will swoop down and sweep all trace of them from the face of
the earth. The Deva hosts will expunge their names from the sacred
Dharma rosters.

I used to assume that I could devote my life to giving the gift
of the Dharma to all people unconditionally and make the teaching
bequeathed by the buddhas of the past flourish once more. How
could I, or anyone, have foreseen the lamentable course that events
have taken? To think that gangs of these wretched bonzes would
wreak damage of this magnitude on the ancient, time-honored practices of their own Dharma ancestors!

You never saw such a wild assortment of sights and scenes! You
would think you were on a battlefield, or gazing at herds of deer
bounding madly over a moor. It would quiver the liver of Fei Lien.
It would set Wu Lai's teeth chattering in panic fear.[4] Arrogance in
all its forms. Every conceivable shade of madness and folly. Not only

do these fellows think nothing of the achievements their predecessors have bequeathed to them, they arrogantly deprive later students of their rightful legacy as well. They are not satisfied until they trample the Dharma banners underfoot and bring the sacred precincts of the temple into total discord.

These are the real Dharma reprobates—the ones to call "hopelessly unteachable." They are heretics masquerading in Buddhist robes. Avatars of the Evil One himself. Incarnations of the archfiend Papiyas stalking the earth.[5] They will take their sins with them even when they die; for they are destined to fall into the dreadful realms of hell, where unspeakable agonies await them. Once that happens, there is no way for them to repent or atone for the terrible wrongs they have committed, even should they want to.

Their teachers or their parents gave them traveling money and sent them out to pursue their study of Zen. If these elders saw the contemptible lives their students or children now lead, do you suppose for a moment they would be pleased?

Recently, seven or eight of my trusted disciples, men with whom I have lived and practiced, combined their efforts in order to get the temple ready for this lecture meeting. They hauled earth, cleared away rubble and stones. They drew water, got the vegetable gardens up to pitch. They endured cold and hunger, experienced full shares of pain and suffering. They started at dawn, their robes wet with dew; the stars were out when they returned. They worked on the monks' quarters, the well, the cooking ovens, the privy and bath house. Ten thousand hardships. Untold difficulties. Why, you broke into a sweat just watching them. Your eyes would swim just hearing about their deeds. And when you think that monks at any other training hall in the land do the same thing . . . A lecture meeting is certainly nothing to be undertaken lightly.

But then, when all these preparations have been made, these misfits, who have not even dirtied their hands, descend upon us, stirring up all kinds of trouble and totally disrupting the meeting. What on earth goes on in the minds of such men? Dragon kings and Devas who stand guard over the Dharma wail out in lamentation. The local earth gods burn with anger and resentment. Monks of this kind have always been around. They have appeared throughout the ages. Yet not a single one of them has been known to live out his natural span unscathed. Even if they don't run foul of their fellow men, there is no way they can escape the retribution of heaven. They are drawing near the three-forked junction.[6] They should be shaking in their sandals.

I have always loathed monks of their type. They are tiger fodder, no doubt about it. I hope one tears them into tiny shreds. The pernicious thieves—even if you killed off seven or eight of them every day, you would still remain totally blameless. Why are we so infested with them? Because the ancestral gardens have been neglected. They have run to seed. The verdant Dharma foliage has withered and only a wasteland remains.

We have in this Zen school of ours an essential Barrier that must be passed through. A forest of thorn and bramble that must be penetrated. But these people don't even know that such things exist. They haven't encountered them in their dreams.

Nowadays, you find worthy senior priests, fully qualified Zen teachers, who are reluctant to take on the responsibility of training a large group of students because it means they will have to deal with these trouble-makers. They would rather retreat to some quiet spot where they can "hide their tracks and conceal their light," and make themselves into winter fans and straw dogs. So even if there is a priest who has achieved a mastery of Zen through authentic practice, he will refuse to accept students no matter how fervently they beg him. Turning his back on their pleas, he is content to live a spare, comfortless existence off by himself, heedless of the privation cold or hunger may bring. After a lifetime of such carefree idleness, he finally wastes away inside a small hermitage in some remote corner of the land.

How keenly it struck home to me! It is priests like these who are to blame! They are the ones responsible for undermining the Dharma banners. It is they who are destroying the true style and practices of the school. I had always detested a priest who would refuse to respond to a student's need, but for a long time I had just gone along without giving any more thought to the matter. Then recently, a group of virtuous priests from various parts got together to do something about the problem. With no small amount of embarrassment, I must report that they came to me! They took me to task for neglecting my teaching responsibilities!

The keen and eager monks hungering for a teacher were greatly encouraged and emboldened by this turn of events. They made their descent upon me. Now they come at me from all quarters, like hordes of wasps rising from a broken nest, like mobs of ants swarming from an anthill to the attack. Some are like white-cheeked infants seeking their mother's breast. Some are like black-hearted ministers set on squeezing the populace dry. I can't come up with an excuse to turn them away. I don't have the strength to keep pushing them off. I find myself pinched into a tight corner, all avenues of escape cut off.

However hard I scrutinize my life, I am unable to come up with any reputation that would need protecting. I haven't achieved anything noteworthy for others to esteem. I am ignorant of poetry. I don't understand Zen. I'm as lumpish and indolent a man as you could find. I drift idly along, doing only what pleases me. I sleep and snore to my heart's content. No sooner do I wake up than I'm nodding off again, like a rice-pounder, deep in daydreams. You won't discover much resemblance between me and a real Zen teacher. Not one trait for younger monks to emulate. No one is more keenly aware of this than I am. I view these defects of mine with constant loathing, but I don't know what to do about them. I'm afraid I'm a lost cause.

It's easy work for the villainous monks of today to get the best of a bumbling, good-for-nothing blind old bonze like me. They could disrupt the meeting, throw it into confusion, even cause it to break up early. If that happens, I'll just wait until they have gone, have someone clean up, then I'll close up shop and resume my slumber where I left off. It won't plunge me into despair.

Of course, on the other hand, if thanks to the efforts of my veteran disciples we are able to get through the meeting without incident, that is just fine—but it won't send me into transports of joy. I have no great desire to think up comments for Zen texts. I am not all that keen on sitting and lecturing from the high seat. I'm just hoping the worthy masters around the country, some of them former comrades, will overlook my shiftless ways and not despise me too much. If one or two of them drop around, I'll take them into the hills behind the temple. We can gather some sticks and fallen leaves, make a fire, and simmer up some tea. It would be nice to enjoy ourselves like that, unburdened with work or responsibilities, talking leisurely over old times. It would be nice to spend a month or two savoring the pleasures of a pure and carefree existence like that.

At the same time, I must admit that there are one or two things I want monks engaged in penetrating the Zen depths to know about.

When the resolve to seek the Way first began to burn in me, I was drawn by the spirits of the hills and streams among the high peaks of Iiyama. Deep in the forests of Narasawa, I came upon a decrepit old teacher living in a mountain hermitage. He was known as Shōju Rōjin, the old master of the Shōju Hermitage.[7] His priestly name was Etan. His Dharma grandfather was Gudō Kokushi; his Dharma father was Shidō Mun'an. Shōju was a blind old bonze, filled with deadly venom. And he was true and authentic to the core.

He was always telling students:

> This Zen school of ours began to decline at the end of the Southern Sung. By the time of the Ming dynasty, the transmission had fallen to earth, all petered out. Now what remains of its real poison is found in Japan alone. Even here there's not much left. It's like scanning a midday sky for stars. As for you, you smelly, blind shavepates, you ragtag little lackwits, you wouldn't be able to stumble on it even in your dreams.

Another time, he said:

> You're imposters, the whole lot of you. You look like Zen monks, but you don't understand Zen. You remind me of the clerics in the teaching schools, but you haven't mastered the teachings. Some of you resemble precepts monks, but the precepts are beyond you. There's even a resemblance to the Confucians, but you certainly haven't grasped Confucianism either. What are you really like? I'll tell you. Large sacks of rice, fitted out in black robes.

Once he told us this story:

> There is a Barrier of crucial importance. Before it sit a row of stern officials, each of whom is there to test the ability of those who come to negotiate the Barrier. Unless you pass their muster, you don't get through.
>
> Along comes a man who announces that he is a wheelwright. He sits down, fashions a wheel, shows it to the officials, and they

let him pass. Another person walks up. An artist. He pulls out a brush, paints a picture for them, and is ushered through the gates. A singing girl is allowed to pass after she sings a refrain from one of the current songs. She is followed by a priest of one of the Pure Land sects. He intones loud invocations of the *nembutsu*—"Namu-amida-butsu, Namu-amida-butsu." The gates swing open and he proceeds on his way.

At this point, another man appears. He is clothed in a black robe and declares he is a Zen monk. One of the guardians of the Barrier remarks that "Zen is the crowning pinnacle of the buddhas' Way." He then asks, "What is Zen?"

All the monk can do is to stand there, in a blank daze, looking like a pile of brushwood. The officials take one look at the nervous sweat pouring from under his arms and write him off as a rank imposter, a highly suspicious and totally undesirable character. He winds up as a poor devil of an outcast, condemned to a wretched existence outside the Barrier. What a pitiful turn of events.

Shōju also told us:

At some future date you men will probably have temples of your own. Suppose that you receive an invitation from one of your parishioners, asking you to visit him at his home. You arrive with your head monk and some of your students and are ushered into a large room. You find layers of thick, soft cushions to sit upon; dishes filled with rare delicacies are arranged before you. You sit there in high spirits, partaking of the food without a single qualm, because you believe that as a senior priest such hospitality is something you are rightfully entitled to. You finish eating and are enjoying yourself immensely amid the loud talk and boisterous laughter. Suddenly, one of the people present addresses you. He brings up a difficult point of Zen—the kind that would bring deep furrows to the brow of any Zen monk. He casually suggests that you explain it. At that moment, what kind of response are you going to make? Your heart will probably start to thump wildly in your chest. Your body will break out in a muck sweat. Your distress will cast a black pall over the entire room.

So inasmuch as you are members of the Zen school, you should concentrate earnestly on your training. If you don't, you will be unwittingly sowing the seeds of your own shame and disgrace. There's no telling when you will be placed in such a harrowing predicament. It's too terrifying to even contemplate.

He also said:

In recent times, monks are given the Mu koan to work on.[8] With diligence and concentration, one man among them—or half a man—may be passed by his master.[9] But in achieving this first small breakthrough, the student forgets about his teacher. He gets the idea that he has enlightened himself and goes around crowing about it to anyone who will listen—sure signs that he is still confined within samsara. Then he proceeds to hatch ideas of his own on various matters pertaining to Zen. With cultivation, these grow and prosper. But the gardens of the patriarchs are still beyond his farthest horizons.

If you want to reach the ground where true peace and comfort is found, the more you realize, the harder you will strive. The further you reach, the further you will press forward. When you finally do see the ultimate truth of the patriarchal teachers, there will be no mistake about it—it will be as if it is right there in the palm of your hand. Why is this? You don't trim your nails at the foot of a lamp.[10]

There is a rich family in eastern Shinano province. They amassed their great wealth over several generations, until their influence rivaled that of the provincial daimyo himself. Their residence is so spacious, the family so large, a bell is needed at mealtime to call everyone together. Occasionally they receive visits from the great and powerful, but on the whole they live a quiet, comfortable, and unobtrusive life. No one even seemed to know what the family business was. Then, in recent years, a large number of young servants were added to the staff. They erected a row of water mills that can be heard grinding away day and night. A procession of rice carts can always be seen trundling in through the gates. They are ten times more prosperous than they were before. It is rumored that they brew almost two hundred thousand liters of sake daily.

An old man living nearby observed these developments. He said: "Mark my words, the prosperity of that house won't last much longer. What you see now are signs of the end approaching. When things deteriorate internally, the external aspect always tends to swell out like that. They may turn to selling rice for a time, or medicinal herbs, and try to save the situation. But you'll see before long that they'll be forced to put the family house up for sale."

When Shōju heard the old man's prediction, he heaved a heavy sigh. "Is that what he said? Our Zen school has been in constant decline from the time of the Sung. It has continued on up until the fall of the Ming. Yet the training halls were always full and seemingly prosperous. It's just as the old man said."

When he finished speaking, his eyes were filled with tears.

I have recorded a few brief examples of old Shōju's instructions as I remember them, in the hope that they will give you an idea of the anger, the scoldings and verbal abuse, the shouts of encouragement, that he used in his daily teaching, as well as a sense of the deep concern and sad regrets he often voiced about the present state of the Zen school.

2

THE POISONOUS LEAVINGS OF
PAST MASTERS

Priest Ch'ien-feng addressed his assembly:

"This Dharma-body has three kinds of sickness and two kinds of light. Can any of you clarify that?"

Yün-men came forward and said, "Why doesn't the fellow inside the hermitage know what's going on outside?"

Ch'ien-feng roared with laughter.

"Your student still has his doubts," Yün-men said.

"What are you thinking of?" said Ch'ien-feng.

"That's for you to clarify," said Yün-men.

"If you're like that," Ch'ien-feng said, "I'd say you're home free."[1]

Anyone who wants to read old Hsi-keng's *Records* must first penetrate these words spoken by Zen masters Ch'ien-feng and Yün-men. If you can grasp the meaning of the dialogue that passed between these two great Zen masters, you are free to say, "I have seen old Hsi-keng face to face. I have penetrated the hidden depths."

If, on the other hand, you cannot grasp it, even though you master the secrets of Zen's Five Houses and Seven Schools and penetrate the inner meaning of all seventeen hundred koans, your understanding

will be nothing but empty theory. Lifeless learning. It will be no use
to you whatsoever.

As for the various practices modern-day students have fallen into,
such as writing down idle, nonsensical speculations they hear from
their deadbeat teachers, or copying notes that others have made, past-
ing such notes as cribs in the margins of Zen texts, glibly passing
information of this kind around to others, embellished for good measure with arbitrary observations of their own—need I mention how
useless those pastimes are?

During the last century, a Chinese priest named Yüan-hsien Yung-
chiao [active during the Ch'ung-chen period, 1628–1644, of the Ming
dynasty] offered an interpretation of this dialogue, but his comments
are so far off the mark they not only misconstrue Ch'ien-feng's meaning, they are a gross insult to Yün-men as well.

Today's priests will take one of the verse comments Hsi-keng
wrote on this dialogue, throw in a few of Yung-chiao's remarks ran-
domly, and then use it when they give Zen lectures in their temples.
With that, they assume they have pronounced the final word on the
subject. They will even commit their comments to paper, and pass
them to their monks. These students, whose eyes are still unopened,
have no idea that what they are being given is a load of stinking filth
that will bury their true spirit, a dangerous weapon that will wreak
mortal injury upon the vital wisdom that is within them.

Yet monks scramble over one another to get their hands on these
notes. They make copies of them, treasure them, keep them a dark
secret, and never let others near them. They transfer the comments
onto small slips of paper and paste them as glosses into the printed
pages of Zen writings, ridiculously supposing that it will help them
to understand the true meaning of the text.

One of these slips of paper that I happened to see was inscribed as
follows:

> In the fourth chapter of a collection of Zen records titled *Ch'an-yü
> nei-chi* is a Dharma talk [*fusetsu*] the Ming priest Yung-chiao gave
> to his assembly during the December practice session:
>
> Ch'ien-feng says that the Dharma-body has three kinds of sick-
> ness and two kinds of light; he also says that there is an opening

through which to pass beyond these obstructions. Now, even if I have to lose my eyebrows for doing it, I'm going to explain the true meaning of Ch'ien-feng's words to you.[2]

As a rule, mountains, streams, the great earth, light and darkness, form and emptiness, and all the other myriad phenomena obstruct your vision and are, as such, impediments to the Dharma-body. That is the first of the sicknesses Ch'ien-feng refers to.

When you go on to realize the emptiness of all things and begin dimly to discern the true principle of the Dharma-body, but are unable to leave your attachment to the Dharma behind—that is the second sickness.

When you are able to bore through and attain the Dharma-body, but you realize upon investigating it anew that there is no way to grasp hold of it, no way to postulate it or to indicate it to others, attachment to the Dharma still remains. That is the third sickness.

The first sickness is a kind of light that doesn't penetrate freely. The second and third sicknesses are likewise a kind of light; it doesn't penetrate with unobstructed freedom either.

When a student has bored his way through the opening mentioned, he is beyond these obstructions and is able to see clearly the three sicknesses and two lights, with no need for even the slightest bit of further effort.

Complete nonsense! Discriminatory drivel of the first water. When I read that, my hands involuntarily closed the book. Doubting my own eyes, I shut them and sat there, utterly appalled. How could anyone believe such feeble remarks are capable of clarifying the ultimate principle of Zen?

Yün-men said, "Why doesn't the fellow inside the hermitage know what's going on outside?" What principle does *that* expound? How are you going to annotate it? Don't for a moment think: "I've penetrated Ch'ien-feng's meaning, but I can't understand what Yün-men means." The utterances exchanged between these two great and worthy old teachers are a pair of peerless swords slanting upward into the sky. They are the sharp fangs of a ferocious tiger, the trunk of the elephant king, the milk of the lion, a poison drum, the tail of the Chen-bird, a world-ending conflagration. If you falter before them,

have the slightest doubt about them, you will find that you are standing alone on a vast moor littered with white skulls. Utterances like
these are the fangs and claws of the Dharma cave, divine amulets
that rob you of your life. Truly, they stand as timeless examples for
all who dwell in the groves of Zen.

I have heard Yung-chiao praised as an outstanding teacher of Sōtō
Zen. A direct heir of Master Wu-ming Hui-ching of Shou-ch'ang-
ssu Temple, he is said to have achieved great success in reviving the
essentials of master Tung-shan's teaching, and in breathing new life
into the true spirit of the Sixth Patriarch's Zen. He has been called
one of the dragons of his age, the mere mention of whose name
makes people sit up straight in solemn reverence.

If all this is correct, how are we to account for the wild and woe-
fully inadequate utterances we have just read? If the *Ch'an-yü nei-chi*
is really from Yung-chiao's own hand, his Zen attainment was of a
highly dubious nature. Maybe he wasn't to blame. Perhaps someone
else, some irresponsible priests, inserted their own notions surrepti-
tiously into Yung-chiao's work, hoping to gain credit for them by
passing them off as those of an eminent priest.

In any case, anyone who would try to palm off discriminatory
delusions of this ilk as the final reaches of the Zen Way could never
have encountered either old Ch'ien-feng or the great master Yün-
men, not even in his dreams. He doesn't deserve to be called a teacher
of men. He should never imagine that he "has no need for the slightest bit of further effort." However many thousands, ten of thousands,
even millions of bits of further effort he chose to expend, it would all
be in vain.

In the past, for uttering just two false words—"don't fall"—a man
plunged into the cave-black darkness of a wild fox existence for five
hundred lives.[3] Make no mistake about it: once a teacher allows even
a single erroneous comment to pass from his lips and blinds students
engaged in exploring the Zen depths, his fate is sealed. He has committed a sin of a blacker dye than causing blood to flow from the
bodies of all the buddhas in the ten directions.

When I make these statements, don't think I'm just indulging in
idle criticism, or that I'm motivated by self-interest. The only reason
I do it is because I hate to see these false, deluded views spread, gain

currency, and obstruct later generations of students in their progress toward enlightenment. They are a foul influence that pollutes the true and original essence of the ancients, withers the Zen groves and parches the life from the Zen gardens. What could go through the minds of such men?

It is said that the Zen gardens in China went to seed during the Ming dynasty, so that the true customs and style of the school were choked off completely. I can believe it. Here in our own country the Zen school is on its last legs as well. Truly, it is a horrifying situation.

I want you patricians penetrating Zen's hidden depths to know that these words of instruction Ch'ien-feng addresses to his monks are very difficult—*difficult in the extreme*. You should never think otherwise. Don't be lapping at fox slobber like this mess that Yung-chiao spewed before you just now. Just concentrate yourselves steadily and singlemindedly on gnawing your way into Ch'ien-feng's words. Suddenly, unexpectedly, your teeth will sink in. Your body will pour with cold sweat. At that instant it will all become clear. You will see the infinite compassion contained in Ch'ien-feng's instructions. You will grasp the timeless sublimity of Yün-men's response. You will fully comprehend the essential truth that Hsi-keng captures in his verse. You will know Yung-chiao's explanations for the tissue of absurdities they are and find that you are in total agreement with the verdict I have pronounced on them. What a thrilling moment it will be!

One of the virtuous teachers of the past said:

> Today even a seasoned monk who has experienced the initial stages of realization and has traveled around to study under different teachers will, unless he runs up against the devious, villainous methods of a genuine master, remain firmly entrenched within his own arbitrary views. He may apply himself single-mindedly to pursuing the Way, may keep at it until everything, even his aspiration and all thought for his own well-being, is forgotten, and then continue on reverently, sifting and refining as he goes. But he only succeeds in clothing himself in cherished ideas of his own making, filthy, clinging garments that he will find impossible to strip away. Once the time and conditions are right for him to start teaching others, when he engages them in direct eyeball-to-eyeball confron-

tation, he discovers that he is unable to respond to their thrusts with the easy, spontaneous freedom of a true teacher. This is because he has until now gone along savoring the fruits of his attainment, and his teachers and others have always treated him with kindness and respect. When he encounters students face to face and tries to put his attainment to work, the words just do not come.[4]

This remonstrance seems to have been directed expressly at the kind of false teacher I have been talking about.

From the Zen people of today, who are content to sit quietly submerged at the bottom of their "ponds of tranquil water," you often hear this: "Don't introspect koans. Koans are quagmires. They will suck your self-nature under. Have nothing to do with written words either. Those are a complicated tangle of vines that will grab hold of your vital spirit and choke the life from it."

Don't believe that for a minute! What kind of "self-nature" is it that can be "sucked under"? Is it like one of those yams or chestnuts you bury under the cooking coals? Any "vital spirit" that can be "grabbed and choked off" is equally dubious. Is it like when a rabbit or fox gets caught in a snare? Where in the world do they find these things? The back shelves of some old country store? Wherever, it must be a very strange place.

No doubt about it, these are the miserable wretches Zen priest Ch'ang-sha said "confound the illusory working of their own minds for ultimate truth." They're like that great king master Ying-an T'an-hua talked about, who lives alone inside an old shrine deep in the mountains, never putting any of his wisdom to use.

But the day will surely come when they will be confronted by a fearless monk who is ready to give his life for the Dharma. He will push a tough old koan under one of their noses. Face to face, he will demand, "What does this mean?"

At that instant, do you think the teacher will be able to croak out that line about koans being "quagmires"? Will he be able to say, "Oh, they're a tangle of vines"? No. He will be at an utter loss, unable to spit out any decent response at all. He may try to reply with anger, but it won't have any conviction behind it. Or he may break out and cry, but he won't be able to cry himself out of his difficulties either.

At present, this country is infested with a race of smooth-tongued, worldly-wise Zen teachers who feed their students a ration of utter nonsense. "Why do you suppose buddha-patriarchs through the ages were so mortally afraid of words and letters?" they ask you. "It is," they answer you,

> because words and letters are a coast of jagged cliffs constantly lashed by a vast ocean of poison ready to swallow up your wisdom, drown the very life from it. Giving students stories and episodes from the Zen past and having them try to penetrate their meaning is a practice that did not start until after the school had branched out into the Five Houses and Seven Schools. It was an expedient teaching method, employed provisionally. It doesn't represent the ultimate reaches of the buddha-patriarchs.

An incorrigible pack of skin-headed mules has ridden teachings like these to a position of dominance in the world of Zen. Unable to distinguish master from servant, jades from common stones, they gather together and sit. Rows of sleepy inanimate lumps. They hug themselves, self-satisfied, imagining they are paragons of the Zen tradition, belittling the buddha-patriarchs of the past and treating their fellow priests with contempt. While true celestial phoenixes linger starving in the shadows, a hateful flock of owls and ravens, comfortable and full-bellied, rule the roost.

But without the eye of *kenshō*, they won't be able to use a single drop of the knowledge they gain. When they die, they will fall straight into hell. Hence I say to them: "If upon becoming a Buddhist monk you do not penetrate the Buddha's truth, turn in your black robe. Give back all the donations you've received! Be a layman again!"

Don't you realize that every syllable contained in the Buddhist canon—all five thousand and forty-eight scrolls of it—is a rocky cliff that juts out into deadly, poison-filled seas? Don't you know that each of the twenty-eight buddhas and six Buddhist saints is a body of virulent poison that rises in monstrous waves, blackening the skies, swallowing the radiance of the sun and moon, extinguishing the light of the stars and planets?[5]

It is there, as clear and stark as it could be. It stares you right in the face. But none of you is awake to see it. You are like an owl venturing into the light of day, gazing around with eyes wide open, but unable to see a mountain towering in front of it. It isn't because the mountain bears a grudge against owls and wants to avoid them. The responsibility lies with the owl alone.

You might cover your ears with your hands, or cover your eyes with a blindfold, or try some other means to avoid the poisonous fumes. But you can't escape the clouds that sail in the sky, the streams that tumble down the hillsides. You can't escape the falling autumn leaves and scattering spring flowers.

You could even enlist the services of a swift-winged Yaksha demon. By plying him with the best of food and drink and crossing his paw with gold, you might persuade him to take you on his back for a few quick circumnavigations of the globe. But you would still be unable to find so much as a thimbleful of earth where you could hide.

I eagerly await the appearance of just one dimwit of a monk (or even half such a monk), richly endowed with a natural stock of spiritual power and kindled within by a raging religious fire, who will fling himself unhesitatingly into the midst of this poison and instantly perish into the Great Death. Rising from that Death, he will arm himself with a calabash of gigantic size and roam the great earth seeking out true and genuine monks.[6] Wherever he encounters one, he will spit in his fist, flex his muscles, fill his calabash with deadly poison, and fling a dipperful over the monk. Drenched from head to foot, that monk too will be forced to surrender his life. What a splendid sight to behold!

The teaching Zen priests today are busily imparting to their students sounds something like this:

> Don't misdirect your effort by chasing around looking for something outside yourself. All you have to do is to concentrate on being thoughtless and doing nothing whatever. No practice. No realization. Doing nothing, the state of no-mind, is the direct path to sudden realization. No practice, no realization, is the true principle—things as they really are. The enlightened buddhas of the ten directions have called this supreme, unparalleled, right awakening.

People hear this teaching and try to follow it. Choking off their aspirations, sweeping their minds clean of delusive thoughts, they dedicate themselves to doing nothing but keeping their minds complete blanks, blissfully unaware that they are, in the process, doing and thinking a great deal.

When a person who has not experienced *kenshō* reads the Buddhist scriptures, questions his teachers and fellow monks about Buddhism, or engages in religious disciplines, it is all unenlightened activity, and it demonstrates abundantly that he is still trapped within samsara. He tries constantly to remain detached in thought and deed, but all the while his thoughts and deeds remain attached. He endeavors to be doing nothing all day long, and all day long he is busily doing.

But let this same person experience *kenshō*, and everything changes. Now, though he is constantly thinking and acting, it is all totally free and unattached. Although he is engaged in activity around the clock, that activity is, as such, nonactivity. This great change is the result of *kenshō*. It is like snakes and cows drinking water from the same cistern: it becomes deadly venom in one and milk in the other.

Bodhidharma spoke of this in his *Essay on the Dharma Pulse*:

> If someone without *kenshō* makes a constant effort to keep his thoughts free and unattached, not only is he a great fool, he also commits a serious transgression against the Dharma. He winds up in the passive indifference of empty emptiness, no more capable of distinguishing good from bad than a drunken man. If you want to put the Dharma of nonactivity into practice, you must put an end to all your thought-attachments by breaking through into *kenshō*. Unless you have *kenshō*, you can never expect to attain a state of nondoing.[7]

Zen master Ch'ang-tsung Chao-chüeh of Tung-lin, a Dharma heir of master Huang-lung Hui-nan, used to tell his students:[8] "Senior priests Hui-t'ang and Hsin-ching, fellow students of mine under master Huang-lung, were only able to penetrate our late teacher's Zen. They were unable to attain his Way." Master Ta-hui said:

> Chao-chüeh said that because, for him, attaining the Way meant remaining as he was and doing nothing all the time—keeping thoughts, views, and the like from arising in his mind, instead of seeking beyond that for wondrous enlightenment. He constructed

a teaching out of the Dharma gate of *kenshō*, the true sudden enlightenment of buddha-patriarchs such as Te-shan, Lin-chi, Tung-
shan, Ts'ao-shan, and Yün-men. He took what the *Shurangama
Sutra* says about mountains and rivers and the great earth all being
manifestations that appear within the inconceivable clarity of the
true mind, and rendered it into words devoid of substance—they
were mere constructions erected in his head. In fabricating his Zen
from profound utterances and wondrous teachings of Zen masters
of the past, he blackened the good name of these Dharma ancestors—and he robbed later generations of students of their eyes and
ears. Not a drop of real blood flowed beneath his skin. His eyes
possessed not a shred of strength. He and men like him infallibly
get things turned upside down. Then they forge on, totally unaware, into ever-deeper ignorance. What a pitiful spectacle they
are![9]

In *The Sutra of Perfect Enlightenment* we read that "people in the
latter day of the Dharma, including even those who aspire to attain
the Buddha Way, should not be made to seek enlightenment, for if
they do they will only wind up amassing stores of knowledge and
deepening their self-made delusions."

In the same sutra: "In the latter day, even if sentient beings seek
help from a good teacher, they still end up learning false views. Because of this, they are never able to attain right enlightenment. This
is a proven recipe for heresy. It is the fault of the false teachers, not
the fault of the sentient beings who go to them for help."

Could these statements from a sutra, preached from the mouth of
the Buddha, be merely empty words?

It was this very question that prompted priest Hsin-ching to declare in an informal discourse (*shōsan*) to his monks:

> These days priests everywhere latch on to phrases such as "every-
> day mind is the Way," and set them up as some sort of ultimate
> principle. You hear that "Heaven is heaven," "Earth is earth,"
> "Mountains are mountains," "Streams are streams," "Monks are
> monks," "Lay people are lay people." They tell you that long
> months last thirty days and short ones last twenty-nine. The fact of
> the matter is, not a single one of them is able to stand on his own

two legs. They flit about like disembodied spirits, clinging to trees, leaning on plants and grasses. Unawakened, blinded by ignorance, they plod their blinkered one-track ways.

Confront one of them and suddenly ask, "Why does this hand of mine resemble a buddha's hand?" and he says, "But that's your hand."

Ask him, "How is it my foot is just like a donkey's?" "That's your foot," he retorts.

"Each person has his own circumstances of birth. What are yours, senior priest?" "I am so and so," he responds. "I'm from such and such province."[10]

Now what kind of answers are those? They proceed from a mistaken understanding that should never be allowed. But these people still insist that all you have to do is make yourself one-track like them and remain that way through thick and thin. This, they assure you, is attainment of the final state of complete tranquillity. Everything is settled. Everything is understood. Nothing doubting. Nothing seeking. There is no questioning at all. They refuse to venture a single step beyond this, terrified that they might stumble and fall into a hole or ditch. They tread the long pilgrimage of human life as if blind from birth, grasping their staff with a clutch of death, refusing to venture forward an inch unless they have it along to prop them up.

Priest Hui-t'ang told his students: "Go to Mount Lu [where Chao-chüeh's temple was located] and plant yourselves firmly within the realm of nondoing."

But Chao-chüeh's descendants have all disappeared. It is truly regrettable, but now his line is deader than last night's ashes.

Zen master Nan-t'ung Yüan-ching said, "You must see your own nature *kenshō* as clearly and unmistakably as you see the palm of your hand. At the fundamental ground of your being there must be an undisturbed tranquillity."

I want to impress all patricians who probe the secret depths—great men all—with the need to put your innate power to work for you as vigorously and relentlessly as you can. The moment your *kenshō* is perfectly clear, throw it aside and dedicate yourself to boring through the difficult-to-pass (*nantō*) koans. Once you are beyond those barriers you will understand exactly what the Buddha meant when he said that a buddha can see the buddha-nature with his own eyes as distinctly as you see a fruit lying in the palm of your hand.

Once you penetrate to see the ultimate meaning of the patriarchal teachers, you will be armed for the first time with the fangs and claws of the Dharma cave. You will sport the divine, life-usurping talisman. You will enter into the realm of the buddhas, stroll leisurely through the realms where evil demons dwell, pulling out nails, wrenching free wedges, dispersing great clouds of compassion as you go, practicing the great Dharma giving, and rendering immense benefit to the monks who come to you from the four quarters.

But you will still be the same old monk you always were. You won't be doing anything out of the ordinary. Your eyes will stare out from your face from the same location as before. Your nose will be where it always was. Yet now you will be the genuine article, an authentic descendant of the buddhas and patriarchs, to whom you will have fully repaid that incalculable debt of gratitude which you owe them.

You will be at liberty to spend your days free from the clutches of circumstance. You will drink tea when it is given; eat rice when it is served. Doing and nondoing will be firmly in your grasp. Not even the buddha-patriarchs will be able to touch you. You'll be a true monk, worth alms of millions in gold.

If, on the other hand, you follow the trend of the times, when you enter the dark cave of unknowing in the eighth consciousness,[11] you will start bragging about what you have achieved. You will go around telling everyone how enlightened you are. You will accept, under false pretenses, the veneration and charity of others, and wind up being one of those arrogant creatures who declares he has attained realization when he has not.

Is that the course you choose to follow? If so, a horrifying fate awaits you. Every grain of rice that you have received as a donation will turn into a red-hot particle of iron or a burning grain of sand. Each drop of water you have received will become a speck of molten bronze or boiling excrement. Each thread of the cloth you have accepted will fuse to your body like a flaming wire net or a suit of white-hot chain.

How sad! You have your heads shaved, you put on a black robe, because you hope to free yourselves from the press of birth and death. Then you make the mistake of falling under the spell of a false teacher and you spend the rest of your lives as irresponsible, no-account priests. Nor will it end there. When you finally breathe your last and depart this life, because you will not have learned from the terrible torments you have undergone in your previous existences, you will go right back to your old home in the three evil paths of transmigration. With your Buddhist surplice still hanging around your shoulders, you will fall into the depths of hell and suffer endless torments. You will remain trapped in the cycle of rebirth until your karmic accounts have been settled in full. You can see, then, that nothing is more terrifying than to fall victim to the delusions a false teacher serves up to you.

> Once long ago a group of seven wise sisters was walking through a graveyard on the outskirts of Rajagriha in India. One of the sisters pointed to a corpse and said to the others, "There is a man's body. Where has the man gone?"
>
> "*What!!*" another said in disbelief. "*What did you say!*" With this, the sisters all realized the truth and were instantly enlightened.
>
> Indra, Lord of the Devas, was moved to shower a rain of flowers down upon them. "Tell me," he said to them, "if there is anything that any of you holy ladies desire; I will see that you have it as long as I am here."[12]

Today's irresponsible Zennists should take a hard look at this story. If their refusal to have anything to do with words is valid, the realization these ladies attained long ago must have been false. But why would the Lord of Devas have spoken to them as he did if their realization was not genuine?

> In response to Indra's offer, one of the sisters said, "None of us lack the four basic necessities of life. We possess the seven rare treasures as well.[13] But there are three things we desire from you. Please give us a tree without roots; some land where there is neither light nor shade; and a mountain valley where a shout does not echo."
>
> "Ask anything else, ladies," replied Indra, "I will gladly provide it. But to be truthful, I just don't have those things to give you."

"If you don't have them," said the woman, "how can you possibly expect to help others liberate themselves?" Indra finally took the young women to visit the Buddha.

Do you see what that wise young woman said? "If you don't have them, how do you expect to save others?" Compare that with the fellows today who shrink back cringing, quaking with fear, when someone confronts them with a dash or two of poison. How infinitely superior she is—the difference between a crown and an old shoe is not nearly so great.

You monks set out on your religious quest with fire in your blood. You go through great difficulties, suffer untold hardships, as you bore into the secret depths of Zen. Isn't it all because you intend at some later date to do great work by bringing the benefits of salvation to your fellow beings? What about you? Don't you think you'd be lacking if you couldn't come up with these three things?

> When the Buddha learned why Indra had come, he said, "As far as that's concerned, Indra, none of the *arhats* in my assembly has the slightest clue either. It takes a great bodhisattva to grasp it."

Why did the Buddha utter these words, instead of quaking and quivering with fear? Or do you suppose he was unaware of the deadly poison contained in the woman's utterance?

Try to fathom the Buddha's intent here. Don't you think he was hoping to make Indra realize the true meaning of the young woman's words? To enable him to leap directly beyond the gradual steps of four attainments and three ranks and arrive at the stage of the great bodhisattvas?

> The Buddha said, "I have the treasure of the true Dharma eye, the exquisite mind of nirvana, the Dharma gate of the true formless form. This I entrust to you, Kashyapa."

This is another statement most people get totally wrong. Years ago, when I was studying with old Shōju, he would give me a koan to work on, and then he would push me and hound me ruthlessly. When I produced a response, he would reward it with a rain of blows from his staff. Thanks to that, I was able to break through and come up with an answer. But I still really wasn't there. I was like a man out at sea gazing at a tree on a distant cliff.

I left home to become a Buddhist monk when I was fourteen. I became discouraged before even a year was out. My head had been shaved smooth, I wore a black robe, but I hadn't seen any sign of the Dharma's marvelous working. I happened to hear that *The Lotus Sutra* was the king of all the scriptures the Buddha had preached. It was supposed to contain the essential meaning of all the buddhas. I got hold of a copy and read it through. But when I had finished, I closed it with a heavy sigh. "This," I told myself, "is nothing but a collection of simple tales about cause and effect. True, mention is made of there being 'only one absolute vehicle,' and of 'the changeless, unconditioned tranquillity of all dharmas,' but on the whole it is what Lin-chi dismissed as 'mere verbal prescriptions for relieving the world's ills.'[14] I'm not going to find what I'm looking for here."

I was deeply disillusioned. I didn't get over it for quite some time. Meanwhile, I lived as the priest of a small temple. I reached forty, the age when one is not supposed to be bothered any longer by doubts. One night, I decided to take another look at *The Lotus Sutra*. I got out my only lamp, turned up the wick, and began to read it once again. I read as far as the third chapter, the one on parables. Then, just like that, all the lingering doubts and uncertainties vanished from my mind. They suddenly ceased to exist. The reason for the *Lotus*'s reputation as the "king of sutras" was now revealed to me with blinding clarity. Teardrops began cascading down my face like two strings of beads—they came like beans pouring from a ruptured sack. A loud involuntary cry burst from the depths of my being and I began sobbing uncontrollably. And as I did, I knew without any doubt that what I had realized in all those satoris I had experienced, what I had grasped in my understanding of those koans I had passed—had all been totally mistaken. I was finally able to penetrate the source of the free, enlightened activity that permeated Shōju's daily life. I also knew beyond doubt that the tongue in the World-honored One's mouth moved with complete and unrestricted freedom. I realized I richly deserved a good thirty hard blows of the staff, just like Lin-chi!

> Long ago, Ananda asked Kashyapa, "Apart from the transmission robe of gold brocade, what Dharma did the World-honored One entrust to you?"
>
> "Ananda," replied Kashyapa, "go and take down the banner at the gate."

To penetrate to an understanding of these words uttered by Kashyapa is extremely difficult. They are like angry bolts of lightning striking against a granite cliff, tearing it apart. They send sages of the three ranks scattering in panic, they strike terror into the hearts of those of the four attainments. Yet the sightless, shave-pated bonzes inhabiting today's temples expatiate knowingly on them: "The banner at the gate, raised to announce a preaching, stands for what is intermediate and prior to the ultimate principle. Taking down the banner means the Great Matter is achieved." This is an excellent example of the kind of commonplace understanding produced from deluded thinking. It's like when blind men attempt to distinguish colors.

First Zen patriarch Bodhidharma's injunction to "cease all external involvements without; avoid seeking internal peace within," is likewise frequently explained and interpreted on a level of ordinary discriminatory reasoning.

> At the end of his life, Hui-neng, the sixth patriarch of Zen after Bodhidharma, was asked by one of his disciples: "You will leave us soon. How long will it be before you come back to us?"
>
> He replied, "Leaves fall and return to the roots. When they appear again, they are silent."

Terrifying! A bottomless pit, ten thousand leagues wide, filled with a sea of intense black flame. Here even the gods and demons cannot hope to complete their lives. The whole world is truly the "lotus-blue eye of the Zen monk." We must be very careful not to throw sand in it.

Yet the know-it-all dunces in positions of power today declare smugly: "Roots refers to the Sixth Patriarch's native place in Hsin-chou. The silence of the leaves points to the original field of tranquility, where no coming or going, no inside or outside, obtains."

Pffuph! Blind comments. Lifeless, perverted understanding. I get sick to my stomach every time I see or hear such rubbish. It makes you want to vomit.

> They asked the Sixth Patriarch, "Who have you entrusted with your Dharma?" He answered, "Take a net and snare it at the top of Ta-yü Peak."

Chen-bird feathers! Wolf liver! Cat heads! Fox drool![15] All brothed up in a large pot and thrown right under your nose. How will you get your teeth into that? Let no one ever say the Sixth Patriarch doesn't have any poison.

> The great teacher Nan-yüeh said, "Suppose an ox is pulling a cart, and the cart doesn't move. Should you hit the cart? Or should you hit the ox?"[16]

Nan-yüeh's words are also filled with poison of the most virulent kind. Yet these modern exegetes insist on applying their deluded reasoning to them: "The cart stands for the body or substance. The ox stands for something intermediate, neither this nor that." They certainly make it sound plausible.

When they hear Master Ma-tsu's "Sun-faced Buddha, moon-faced Buddha," they tell you that it is "the body of one's proper subtle radiance that is prior to the onset of all the illnesses of mind." And they expect you to swallow it! You could take a conventional explanation like this, knead it up with some good rice, and stick it out under the trees for a thousand days without getting even a crow to fly by for a second look.

3

AUTHENTIC ZEN

When a son of the Shakya clan (known later as the "golden sage") went into the fastness of the Snowy Mountains long ago to begin his first retreat, he cradled secretly in his arms an ancient, stringless lute.[1] He strummed it with blind devotion for over six years until, one morning, he saw a beam of light shining down from a bad star, and was startled out of his senses.[2] The lute, strings and all, shattered into a million pieces. Presently, strange sounds began to issue from the surrounding heavens. Marvelous tones rose from the bowels of the earth. From that moment, he found that whenever he so much as moved a finger, sounds came forth that wrought successions of wondrous events, enlightening living beings of every kind.[3]

It began in the Deer Park, where he strummed an old four-strutted instrument from which issued twelve elegant tones. In midcareer, at Vulture Peak, he articulated the perfectly rounded notes of the One Vehicle. At the end, he entered the Grove of Cranes, and from there the sad strains of his final song were heard.[4] His repertoire reached a total of five thousand and forty scrolls of marvelously wrought music.

A person appeared who understood. He could grasp these notes at the touch of a single string. He was known as Great Turtle. When his carapace fractured—a sudden blossom-burst of cracks and fissures—the melody was taken up on the strings of twenty-eight mighty instruments. The last of them was a divine, blue-eyed virtuoso with a purple beard. How wonderful he was! With one sweep of the lion strings he swallowed up the voices of all the six schools. Eight times the phoenix strings sang out; eight times the divine lute passed in secret transmission. The source of it all was this man from the land of Kōshi, in south India, who was born the son of a king.[5]

When he reached the forested peaks of the Bear's Ears, he amused himself playing on a holeless iron flute. The sounds were magnificent, but he found they were unable to rend people to their deepest souls, so he parceled out his own skin, flesh, bone, and marrow instead.[6]

Seven steps after him, the transmission stumbled, and a blind lifeless old nag was loosed upon the world.[7] He reared up on his hind legs, pawing the air in high spirits. With his three hundred and sixty joints lathered up, throwing deadly milk wildly in all directions and showers of blood and sweat steaming violently up through his eighty-four thousand pores, he stomped the trichilocosmic universe into dust, he smashed the vaults of heaven into atoms with deafening neighs, striking such panic into millions of Mount Sumerus they toppled over each other trying to escape, and he ravaged every land in the six directions, leaving them strewn behind in tiny pieces.

These sounds carried to the foot of Mount Nan-ch'üan, where a divine celestial drum took up the beat of its own accord. Ch'ang-sha and Chao-chou fell into harmony with the mysterious direct pointing and broke into powerful personal renditions of the secret melody. It reached an old ferryman at the Ta-i Ford, who liked to pass the time tapping away on the sides of his boat. He rapped out rough, barbaric tunes that drowned out the notes of more graceful singers.[8]

Old Elephant Bones sustained the resonance with his wild dances and uncouth ways. At Mount Lo and Mount Su the old tunes, infused with the divine, flowed out in elegant numbers that were regulated perfectly to the Dharma truth. Shou-shan and Tz'u-ming pitched their melodies to the tones of "yellow bell" and "great harmony," making music that was soft and subtle, yet so stern and unyielding it set country demons scuttling in horror and idle spirits scurrying into hiding.[9]

The sternest, most trenchant notes that came from the holeless flute reached the abbot's chambers at the Kuang-t'ai-yüan in Kuang-nan province, where a poison drum was slung upside down. From that drum emerged sounds that drained men's souls and burst men's livers, littering the landscape with the bodies of over eighty men, and striking who knows how many others deaf and mute.[10]

Hsiao-ts'ung restrung the lute and carried it up into the fastnesses of Mount Tung. Ch'ung-hsien clasped it to his bosom and entered Mount Hsüeh-tou.[11] From these pinnacles emanated sounds that shook the whole world.

Roarings of an iron lion were heard over the lands west of the river—they would have killed the spirit in a wooden man. Bayings of a straw dog filled the skies over Lake Tzu—they would have started hard sweat on the flanks of a clay ox.[12]

Another true man emerged. He was a son of the Tung family of Pa-hsi in Mien-chou. Known as Tung-shan Lao-jen, the Old Man of the Eastern Mountain, he devoted himself as a young monk to austere religious discipline at Brokenhead Peak. Later, he concealed his presence inside a clump of white cloud. One morning, he entered a rice-hulling shed, tucked up his hemp robe, and made a single circumambulation of the millstone. The thunder from this voiceless cloth drum rolled angrily out, snarling and snapping, and filled the world with far-reaching reverberations. You would have thought the thunder god himself had been hired to pound a poison drum. It rendered three Buddhas utterly senseless, and it drained all the courage from a quiet man.[13]

Ta-hui chanted—his voice reached up and down the coasts of Heng-yang. Wu-chun roared—the reports pierced the bottom of the Dragon Pool. Long howls emanating from Hu-ch'iu, Tiger Hill, shook whole forests to their roots. Bitter, soul-rending cries from a Yellow Dragon checked sailing clouds in their tracks.[14]

Ying-an, Mi-an, Sung-yüan, and Yün-an beat time in conformity to the age-old rhythms with a finesse that placed them head and shoulders above their contemporaries.[15]

An old farmer in Ssu-ming, who called himself Hsi-keng, Resting Farmer, kept up a constant stream of song as he swung his iron mattock. One day, when he saw an ancient column of light emanate from a large peak and illuminate a memorial tower, the marvelous principle entered his fingertips, inspiring them to move across the strings.

Shakyamuni Leaving the Mountains

"Zen practice pursued within activity is a million times superior to that pursued within tranquillity."

Zen Master Lin-chi

Zen Master Hsi-keng (Sokkō)

Hakuin as Hotei, Doing Zazen

Dragon Staff. Hakuin sometimes gave paintings of such staffs to people to certify they had passed a koan—often the koan "What is the sound of the single hand?"

"Mu"

"If you are not there for even an instant, you are just like a dead person."

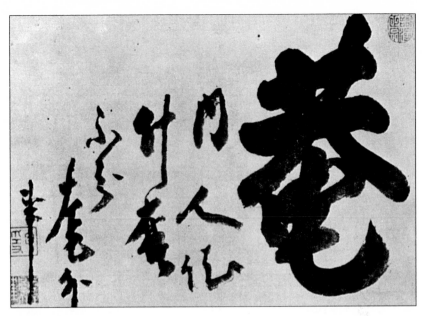

"Why doesn't the fellow inside the hermitage know what's going on outside?"

Mt. Fuji from Shoin-ji Temple

"Perseverance"

The sounds produced shook two forests to their roots, and swept through ten temples.[16]

Echoes from these sounds, floating eastward, landed in Japan. They startled the golden cock, who clapped his wings and announced the coming dawn, while a jade tortoise sobbed out the sorrows of his heart.[17] They brought fine spring warmth to Recumbent Mountain, they danced white flakes of snow over Purple Fields, they sent an auspicious herd of deer darting by so swiftly they made lightning seem slow, and made a bright pearl turn in emptiness with a brilliance that threw the surrounding world into total darkness.[18]

From there, the music wafted into the flower fields of Hanazono. Eight sounds rang out in succession, striking everyone who heard them speechless—they worked like the great poison-lacquered crocodile drum that destroys all within earshot. Branching out, it formed into four main pillars at Myōshin-ji—large instruments that yielded slow, resonant tones, and smaller ones that played with a quicker and more animated beat.[19] Together, their voices rolled throughout the universe, penetrated far beyond the seas.

How sad to see music of such great purity and elegance forgotten, its place taken by these obscene noises pouring forth unchecked. Time-honored classics have been drowned out by the discord these vulgar, degenerate songs produce.

Look at the extraordinary caliber of the patriarchal teachers we have surveyed. How many people today bear any resemblance to them? Most of them have yet to pass through the barrier-koans raised by these illustrious teachers, so the essential core of truth contained in them remains unpenetrated, and the fire still burns restlessly in their minds. They won't have a moment's peace as long as they live. They are like someone who suffers at daily intervals from chronic fever. They try to meditate for five days or so, then they give it up and begin prostrating themselves in front of Buddhist images. Five days later, they give that up too, and start chanting sutras. They keep that up for five days or so, and then switch to a dietary regimen, one meal a day. They are like someone confined to bed with a serious illness who can't sleep and tries to sit up, only to find he is unable to do that either. They stumble ahead like blind mules, not knowing where their feet are taking them. And all because they were careless at the start of their training and were never able to achieve a breakthrough of intense joy and fulfillment.

It frequently happens that someone will take up Zen and spend three, five, perhaps seven years doing zazen, but because he does not apply himself with total devotion he fails to achieve true single-mindedness, and his practice does not bear fruit. The months and years pass, but he never experiences the joy of nirvana, and samsaric retribution is always there waiting if he stops or regresses. At that point, he turns to the calling of Amida's name and goes all he knows for the *nembutsu,* eagerly desirous of being reborn in the Pure Land, abandoning his erstwhile resolve to negotiate the Way and to bore his way through to the truth. In China, people of such pedigree began to emerge in great numbers beginning in the Sung dynasty; they continued to appear up through the Ming and on into the present day. They have most of them been of mediocre caliber, weak, limp-spirited Zennists.

Anxious to cover up their own failure and lessen their sense of shame, they are quick to cite the rebirth in the Pure Land of Zen priests such as Chieh of Mount Wu-tsu, Hsin-ju Che, and I of Tuan-ya, and from their examples draw the conclusion that practicing zazen is ineffective.[20] What they don't seem to know is that those men were primarily followers of the *nembutsu* from the start. Alas! in their eagerness to gain support for their own preconceived and commonplace notions, they rustle up a broken-down reincarnated old warhorse or two whose dedication to Zen practice was weak to begin with, who hadn't gained even a glimpse of the discernment that comes with *kenshō,* and they attempt to throw into disrepute the wise saints who have forged the actual living links in the Dharma transmission. They thus pervert the secret, untransmittable essence that these saints have personally transmitted from Dharma father to Dharma son. The gravity of their offenses exceeds that of the five deadly sins. There is no possible way for them to repent.

Basically, there is no Pure Land existing apart from Zen; there is no mind or Buddha separate from Zen. The Sixth Patriarch Hui-neng manifested himself as a teacher of men for eighty successive lives.[21] The venerable master Nan-yüeh was an embodiment of all three worlds—past, present, and future. They were great oceans of infinite calm and tranquillity, great empty skies where no trace remains, within which there is human rebirth, birth in the Pure Land divine birth—and also the unborn. The joyful realm of paradise, the terrifying hells, the impure world, and the Pure Land are facets manifested by a wish-fulfilling *mani* gem moving freely and easily on a tray. If even the slightest thought to grasp it appears, you become like the foolish man who tried to catch a dragon by scooping up water from a riverbank.

If the First Patriarch, Bodhidharma, had thought the Buddhadharma's ultimate principle was the aspiration for rebirth in the Pure Land, he could have simply sent a letter to China, one or two lines, telling everyone: "Attain rebirth in the Pure Land by devoting yourselves single-mindedly to repeating the *nembutsu*." What need would there have been for him to cross ten thousand miles of perilous ocean, enduring all the hardships he did, in order to transmit the Dharma of seeing into self-nature [*kenshō*]?

Aren't the people who think the Pure Land exists apart from Zen aware of the passage in *The Meditation Sutra* that declares the body of Amida Buddha to be as tall as "ten quadrillion miles multiplied by the number of sand particles in sixty Ganges rivers"?[22] They should reflect on that passage. Give it careful scrutiny. If this meditation on the buddha-body is not the way of supreme enlightenment, of enlightening the mind by seeing into your self-nature, then what is it?

The Pure Land patriarch Eshin Sōzu said, "If your faith is great, you will see a great buddha." Zen practice has you break through so you encounter that venerable old buddha face to face and see him with perfect clarity. When you try to find him somewhere else apart from your self, you join the ranks of the evil demons who work to destroy the Dharma. Hence the Buddha says in *The Diamond Sutra*: "If you see your self as a form or appearance, or seek your self in the voice you hear, you are on the wrong path, and will never be able to see the Buddha."

All tathagatas, or buddhas, are possessed of three bodies: the Dharma-body, Birushana, which is said to be "present in all places"; the Recompense-body, Rushana, which is called "pure and perfect"; and the Transformation-body, Shakyamuni, described as "great perseverance through tranquillity and silence." In sentient beings the three appear as tranquillity, wisdom, and unimpeded activity. Tranquillity corresponds to the Dharma-body, wisdom to the Recompense-body, activity to the Transformation-body.[23]

The great teacher Bodhidharma said,

> If a sentient being constantly works to cultivate good karmic roots, the Transformation-body buddha will manifest itself. If he cultivates wisdom, the Recompense-body buddha will manifest itself. If he cultivates nonactivity, the Dharma-body buddha will manifest itself. In the Transformation-body the buddha soars throughout the ten directions, accommodating himself freely to circumstances as he liberates sentient beings. In the Recompense-body the buddha entered the Snowy Mountains, eliminated evil, cultivated good, and attained the Way. In the Dharma-body, the buddha remains tranquil and unchanging, without words or preaching.
>
> Speaking from the standpoint of the ultimate principle, not even one buddha exists, much less three. The idea of three buddha-bodies only came into being as a response to differences in people's intellectual capacities. People of inferior intellectual capacity, who mistakenly strive to gain benefit from performing good deeds, mistakenly see the buddha of the Transformation-body. Those of mediocre capacity, who mistakenly attempt to cut off their evil passions, mistakenly see the buddha of the Recompense-body. Those of higher intelligence, who mistakenly strive to realize enlightenment, mistakenly see the buddha of the Dharma-body. People of the highest intelligence, however, who illuminate themselves within, attain the perfect tranquillity of the enlightened mind, and are, as such, buddhas. Their buddhahood is attained without recourse to the workings of mind.
>
> Know from this that the three buddha-bodies, and all the myriad phenomena as well, can none of them be either grasped or expounded.
>
> Isn't this what the sutra means when it states that "buddhas do not preach the Dharma, do not save sentient beings, do not realize enlightenment?"[24]

The great teacher Huang-po said,

> The Dharma preaching of the Dharma-body cannot be found in words, sounds, forms, or appearances; it cannot be understood by

means of written words. It is not something you can preach; it is not something you can realize. It is self-nature and self-nature alone, absolutely empty, and open to all things. Hence *The Diamond Sutra* says, "There is no Dharma to preach. The preaching of that unpreachable Dharma is what is called preaching the Dharma." Although buddhas manifest themselves in both the Recompense-body and Transformation-body to expound the Dharma in response to various conditions, that is not the true Dharma. Indeed, as a commentary says, "Neither the Recompense- nor Transformation-body is the true buddha, nor is what they preach the true Dharma."[25]

What you must realize is this: although buddhas appear in response to sentient beings in a limitless variety of sizes and shapes, large and small, they never appear except as these three buddha-bodies. In *The Sutra of the Victorious Kings of Golden Light*, we find the words, "In this way you attain supreme enlightenment possessed of the three buddha-bodies. Among the three, Recompense-body and Transformation-body are provisional names. The Dharma-body alone is true and real, constant and unchanging, the fundamental source of the other two."[26]

Hence *The Meditation Sutra*'s preaching is perfectly clear: "The height of the buddha's body is ten quadrillion miles multiplied by the number of sand particles in sixty Ganges rivers." Can someone tell me: Is this colossal body the Recompense-body? Is it the Transformation-body? Or is it the Dharma-body? We saw before that the Recompense- and Transformation-bodies appear to benefit sentient beings in response to their various capacities. Yet how large would a world have to be to accommodate such a buddha? Can you imagine the gigantic size of the sentient beings to whom he would appear? And don't say that because sentient beings in a Pure Land of such size would be correspondingly large, a buddha would have to manifest himself in a large form too. If that were true, wouldn't bodhisattvas, religious seekers, and everyone else who inhabited such a world have to be of similar size as well: "ten quadrillion miles multiplied by the number of sand particles in sixty Ganges rivers"?

A river the size of the Ganges measures forty leagues across; its sands are as fine as the smallest atoms. Not even a god or demon could count the sand in a single Ganges river, or in half a Ganges river—or even, for that matter, the sand in an area ten feet square. And we are talking about the sand in sixty Ganges! The all-seeing eyes of the Buddha himself could not count them. These, in essence, are numbers that cannot be reckoned, calculations beyond calculating. Yet they contain a profound truth which is among the most difficult to grasp of all those in the Buddha's sutras. It is the golden bone and golden marrow of the Venerable Buddha of Boundless Life.

If I had to say anything about it at all, it would be that the sand in those sixty Ganges rivers alludes to the colors and forms, the sounds, and the rest of the six dusts that appear as objects to the six organs of sense.[27] Not one of all the myriad dharmas exists apart from these six dusts. When you fully awaken to the fact that all the dharmas perceived in this way as the six dusts are, in and of themselves, the golden body of the Buddha of Boundless Life in its entirety, you transcend the realm of samsaric suffering right where you stand and become one with supreme perfect enlightenment.

At that moment, everywhere, both east and west alike, is the Land of the Lotus Paradise. The entire universe in all directions, not a pinpoint of earth excepted, is none other than the great primordial peace and tranquillity of Birushana Buddha's Dharma-body. It pervades all individual entities, erasing all their differences, and this continues forever without change.

The Meditation Sutra goes on to say that those who recite the Mahayana sutras belong to the highest class of the highest rank of those who are reborn directly into the Pure Land of Amida, the Buddha of Boundless Life. What is a "Mahayana" sutra? Well, it's not one of those scrolls of yellow paper with the red handles. No, there's no doubt about it, it indicates the buddha-mind that is originally furnished in your own home.

What possible basis could there then be for that foolish talk about Zen practice being ineffective?

In saying these things I am not referring to those wise saints, motivated by the working of the universal vow of great compassion, who wish to extend the benefits of salvation to people of lesser capabilities. They engage in Pure Land practices themselves in order that they may instill a firm desire for Pure Land rebirth in their followers and enable them to acquire a mastery of the triple mind and fourfold practice.[28]

I refer rather to people of the Zen school who, being incapable of devoting themselves single-mindedly to Zen practice, neglect their training and then go around telling others that Zen practice is useless, that you get no results if you devote yourself solely to Zen. A person like that cannot be allowed to escape without undergoing scrutiny of the severest kind. He is like a Chinese scholar who is passed over for government appointment because he fails the imperial examination. Reduced to an ignoble existence, drifting around the country and living on others, he points to the examples of a few government officials who have been dismissed and banished to the provinces as proof of the uncertainty and precariousness of government service. He is himself a failure, yet he insists upon belittling others of genuine worth who have passed the examinations with highest honors. He reminds you of someone who doesn't have the strength to raise his food up to his mouth to eat, yet who insists he isn't eating because the food is bad.

Adding Pure Land to Zen, someone said, is like fixing a tiger with wings.[29] What empty-headed piffle! Zen! Zen! Anyone who would say something like that could never understand Zen, not in his wildest dreams. Why, if you show wise ones of the three ranks or four ranks the slightest glimpse of its working, they topple over in deep shock, their hearts and their livers sapped of spirit. Even saints who have gone beyond them to higher levels of attainment lose all their nerve. The buddha-patriarchs themselves plead for their lives. Zen is not something that has to appropriate expedient teachings like these from other schools to provide for its future generations.

I recently heard about an old clam who has burrowed himself into a riverbank in Naniwa.[30] There he slumbers away in a thousand-year sleep, missing any chance he might have to encounter a tathagata when one appears in the world. Somehow, however, these words reached his sleeping ears. He raised himself up in a sleepy huff, sprayed out ten thousand bushels of venomous poison foam, opened his jaws wide, and said, "Adding Pure Land to Zen is like depriving a cat of its eyes. Adding Zen to Pure Land is like raising a sail on the back of a cow."[31] The ravings of a sleep-drunk man? Yet even so, such marvelous ravings they are!

Twenty years ago, a man said that in two or three hundred years all Zennists will have joined the Pure Land schools.[32] My answer is, "If a follower of Zen does not devote himself single-mindedly to his practice, he will indeed gravitate to the Pure Land teaching. If a follower of the Pure Land does the *nembutsu* single-mindedly and is able to achieve samadhi, he will inevitably wind up in Zen."

I was once told this story by a great and worthy person:[33] There were, thirty or forty years ago, two holy men. One was named Enjo and the other Engū. It's not known where Engū was from or what his family name was, but he devoted himself constantly and single-mindedly to the calling of Amida's name—he kept at it as relentlessly as he would have swept at a fire on top of his head. One day, he suddenly entered samadhi and realized complete and perfect emancipation. His attainment radiated from his entire being. He immediately set out for Hatsuyama in Tōtōmi province to see old master Tu-chan.[34] When he arrived, Tu-chan asked him, "Where are you from?"

"From Yamashiro," Engū replied. "What Buddhism do you practice?" asked Tu-chan. "I'm a Pure Land Buddhist," he said. "How old is the revered Buddha of Boundless Life?" "He's about my age," said Engū. "Where is he right now?" asked Tu-chan.

Engū made his right hand into a fist and raised it slightly. "You are a true man of the Pure Land," said Tu-chan.

This substantiates what I just said about Pure Land followers gravitating inevitably to Zen if they can attain a state of samadhi by repeating *nembutsu* single-mindedly. Unfortunately, Pure Land followers who turn to Zen are harder to find than stars in the midday sky. While followers of Zen who avail themselves of Pure Land practices are more numerous than the stars on a clear night.

Recently someone told me about people who are holding *nembutsu* meetings in remote Zen temples in the country. It seems they set up gongs and bronze drums like the ones they have in the Pure Land temples, and beat on them as they wail out loud choruses of *nembutsu*. They raise such a terrible din they startle the surrounding villages.

It terrifies me to think of that prediction about Zen three hundred years from now. Barring the appearance of some great Zen saint like Ma-tsu or Lin-chi, the situation seems to be beyond remedy. It gives my liver the willies every time I think about it.

So, loyal and valiant patricians of the secret Zen depths, gird the loins of your spirits. Make piles of brushwood your beds! Make adversity your daily ration!

In the third section of *The Platform Sutra*, the one devoted to doubts and questions, the Sixth Patriarch makes the statement, "Considered as a manifestation in form, the Paradise in the West lies one hundred and eight thousand leagues from here, a distance created by the ten evils and eight false practices in ourselves."[35]

Yün-ch'i Chu-hung, a Ming-dynasty priest of recent times who lived in Hang-chou during the Wan-li period (1573–1627), wrote in his commentary on *The Amida Sutra*:[36]

> *The Platform Sutra* mistakenly identifies India with the Pure Land of Bliss. India and China are both part of this defiled world in which we live. If India were the Pure Land, what need would there be for people to aspire toward the eastern quarter or yearn toward the west? Amida's Pure Land of Bliss lies west of here, many millions of buddha-lands distant from this world.[37]
>
> The work we know as *The Platform Sutra* is comprised of records compiled by disciples of the Sixth Patriarch. We have no assurance that what they have recorded is free from error. We must be very careful to keep such a work from beginning students. If it does fall into the hands of those who lack the capacity to understand it, it will turn them into wild demons of destruction. That would be deplorable.

Faugh! Who was this Chu-hung anyway? Some hidebound Confucian? An apologist for the Lesser Vehicle? Maybe a Buddhist of Pure Land persuasion who cast groundless aspersions on this sacred work because he was blind to the profound truth contained in *The Meditation Sutra*? Because he simply did not possess the Dharma eye which would enable him to read sutras? Or maybe he was a cohort of Mara the Destroyer, manifesting himself in the guise of a priest—shaven-headed, black-robed, hiding behind the mask of verbal *prajna*—bent on destroying with his slander the wondrously subtle, hard-to-encounter words of a true Buddhist saint?

These ascriptions seem to fit Chu-hung all too well. Yet someone took exception to them, saying:[38]

There is no reason to wonder about Master Chu-hung. A good look at him shows that he just lacked the eye of *kenshō*; he didn't have the strength that comes from realizing the Buddha's truth. Not having the karma from previous existences to enable him to reach *prajna* wisdom if he continued forward, and being afraid to retreat because of the terrible samsaric retribution he knew awaited him in the next life, he turned to the Pure Land faith. He began to devote himself exclusively to calling Amida's name, hoping that at his death he would see Amida and his attendant bodhisattvas arrive to welcome him to birth in the Pure Land, and in that way would attain the fruit of buddhahood.[39]

So when he happened to open *The Platform Sutra* and read the golden utterances of the Sixth Patriarch expounding the authentic "direct pointing" of the Zen school, and he realized they were totally at odds with the aspirations he had been cherishing, it dashed all his hopes. It was this that made him rouse himself indignantly and put together the commentary we now see, as a means of redeeming the pipsqueak notions he had grown so attached to.

So he was no Confucian, Taoist, or ally of Mara either. He was just a blind priest with a tolerable gift for the written word. We should not be surprised at him. Beginning from the time of the Sung dynasty, people like him have been as common as flax seeds.

If what this person says is in fact true, the course of action that Chu-hung took was extremely ill-advised. We are fortunate that we do have the compassionate instructions of the Sixth Patriarch. Shouldn't we just read them with veneration, believe in them with reverence, and enter into their sacred precincts? What are we to make of a person who would use his minimal literary talent to try to belittle the lofty wisdom and great religious spirit of a man of the Sixth Patriarch's stature? Even granting that to be permissible as long as he is deluding only himself, it is a sad day indeed when he commits his misconceptions to paper and publishes them as a book that can subvert the Zen teaching for untold numbers of future students.

We generally regard the utterances of a sage as being at odds with the notions held by ordinary people; people who are at variance with such utterances we regard as unenlightened. Now, if the words of a sage are no different from the ideas the unenlightened hold to be right and proper, are not those words themselves ignorant and unenlightened, and unworthy of our respect? If the ignorant are not at variance with the words of an enlightened sage, doesn't that make them enlightened men, and as such truly worthy of our reverence?

To begin with, Master Hui-neng was a great master with an unsurpassed capacity for transmitting the Dharma. None of the other seven hundred pupils who studied with the Fifth Patriarch at Mount Huang-mei could even approach him.[40] His offspring cover the earth now from sea to sea, like the stones on a go board or the stars in the heavens. A common hedgerow monk like Chu-hung, whose arbitrary conjectures and wild surmise all come from fossicking around in piles of old rubbish, should not even be mentioned in the same breath as Hui-neng.

Are you not aware, Chu-hung, that Master Hui-neng is a timeless old mirror in which the realms of heaven and hell and the lands of purity and impurity are all reflected equally? Don't you know that they are, as such, the single eye of a Zen monk?[41] A diamond hammer couldn't break it, the finest sword on earth couldn't penetrate it. This is a realm in which there is no coming and going, no birth and death.

The light emitted from the white hair between Amida Buddha's eyebrows, in which five Sumerus are contained, and his blue lotus eyes, which hold the four great oceans, as well as the trees of seven precious gems and pools of eight virtues that adorn his Pure Land, are all shining brilliantly in our minds right now—they are manifest with perfect clarity right before our eyes. The black cord hell, aggregate hell, shrieking hell, interminable hell, and all the rest are, as such, the entire body of Amida, the venerable Sage of Boundless Life, in all his golden radiance.

It makes no difference whether you call it the Shining Land of Lapis Lazuli in the East or the Immaculate Land of Purity in the South; originally, it is all a single ocean of perfect, unsurpassed awakening.[42] As such, it is also the intrinsic nature in every human being.

But even while it is present in them all, each of them views it in a different way, varying according to the weight of individual karma as well as the amount of merit and good fortune each one enjoys.

Those who suffer the terrible agonies of hell see seething cauldrons and white-hot furnaces. Craving ghosts see raging fires and pools of pus and blood. Fighting demons see a violent battle ground of deadly strife. The unenlightened see a defiled world of ignorance and suffering—all thorns and briars, stones and worthless shards—from which they turn in loathing to seek the Land of Purity. Inhabitants of the Deva realms see a wonderful land of brilliant lapis lazuli and transparent crystal. Adherents of the two vehicles see a realm of transition on the path to final attainment. Bodhisattvas see a land of true recompense filled with glorious adornments. Buddhas see an eternal land of tranquil light. How about you Zen monks? *What do you see?*

You must be aware that the jeweled nets of the heavenly realms and the white-hot iron grates in the realms of hell are themselves thousand-layered robes of finest silk; that the sumptuous repasts of the Pure Land paradise and the molten bronze served up to hell-dwellers are, as such, banquets replete with a hundred rare tastes. In all heaven and earth there is only one moon; not two, not three. Yet there is no way for those of ordinary or inferior capacity to know it.

Followers of the patriarch-teachers, monks of superior capacity striving to penetrate the hidden depths, until you release your hold from the edge of the precipice to which you hang, and perish into life anew, you can never enter this samadhi. But the moment you do, the distinction between Dharma principle and enlightened person disappears, differences between mind and environment vanish. This is what the coming of the old buddha to welcome you to the Pure Land is really about. You are those superior religious seekers the sutra says are destined for "the highest rank of the highest rebirth in the Pure Land."[43]

Master Chu-hung, if you do not once gain entrance into the Pure Land in this way, you could pass through millions upon millions of buddha-lands, undergo rebirth eight thousand times over, but it would all be a mere shadow in a dream, no different from the imaginary land conjured up in Han-tan's slumbering brain.[44]

The Zen master Hui-neng stated unequivocally that the ten evils and eight false practices separate us from the Western Paradise. It is a perfectly justified, absolutely authentic teaching. If the countless tathagatas in the six directions manifested themselves in this world all at one time, they could not, do what they may, change a single syllable of it.

Furthermore, Master Chu-hung, if I said to you, "The Western Paradise is eighteen leagues from here," "the Western Paradise is seven feet over there," "the Western Paradise is eighteen inches away," those too would be perfectly justified, absolutely authentic teachings. How will you lay a hand, or foot, on them! When I make those statements, what village do you suppose I am referring to? And if you hesitate or stop to speculate for even a split second, a broken vermilion staff seven feet long stands ready against the wall.

Resentment at finding the Sixth Patriarch's ideas different from your own led you to take a true teacher totally dedicated to the avowed Buddhist goal of universal salvation and portray him as a dunce who does not even know the difference between the Pure Land and India. Do you think that is right?

We can only suppose that some preconception Chu-hung had formed of the Sixth Patriarch led him to think: "It's really a shame that the Sixth Patriarch, with that profound enlightenment of his, was originally a woodcutter from the uncivilized south. Being illiterate, he couldn't read the Buddhist scriptures. He was rude, coarse, ignorant; in fact, he was no different from those countrymen who herd cows, catch fish, and work as menials."[45]

But is it really possible that even such people wouldn't know the difference between the Pure Land and India? Even a tiny child of three believes in the Pure Land and will worship it with a sense of reverence. And we are talking about a great Buddhist teacher, one of those "difficult-to-meet, hard-to-encounter" sages who rarely appear in the world. The great and venerable Master Hui-neng was a veritable udumbara flower, blossoming auspiciously in fulfillment of the prophecies of the Buddhist sages.

This genuinely enlightened man, endowed with the ten superhuman powers of buddhahood, appeared in the world riding upon the vehicle of the universal vow and revealed a secret of religious attainment never preached by any buddha or patriarch before him. It was like the Dragon King entering the all-encompassing ocean, turning its salt water to fresh and with perfectly unobstructed freedom making it fall over all the earth as pure, sweet manna to revive parched wastelands from the ravages of long drought. It was like a rich man entering an immense treasure house, emerging with many articles rarely seen in the world, and distributing them to the cold and hungry, giving them a new lease on life by relieving their need and suffering. Such cases cannot be judged by commonsense standards, nor can they be revealed by unenlightened speculation.

Priests of today have woven themselves into a complicated web of words and letters. After sucking and gnawing on this mess of literary sewage until their mouths suppurate, they proceed to spew out an endless tissue of irresponsible nonsense. Men like that shouldn't be mentioned in the same breath as the Sixth Patriarch.

Shakyamuni Buddha tells us that the Pure Land lies many millions of buddha-lands distant from here. The Sixth Patriarch says the distance is one hundred and eight thousand leagues. Both utterances come from men whose spiritual power—strength derived from great wisdom—is awesomely vast. Their words reverberate like the earth-shaking stomp of the elephant king. They resound like the roar of the lion monarch, bursting the brains of any jackal or other scavenger who shows the slightest hesitation.

Yet Chu-hung delivers the glib judgment that *"The Platform Sutra* mistakenly regards India as the Pure Land of Bliss." "The work we know as *The Platform Sutra,*" he says, "consists of records compiled by disciples of the Sixth Patriarch. We have no assurance that what they have recorded is free from error." On the pretext of being helpful, what Chu-hung is really doing is disparaging the Sixth Patriarch.

In the *Rokusodankyō kōkan,* a commentary on *The Platform Sutra,* the author writes: "According to gazeteers and geographical works I have consulted, the distance from the western gate of Ch'ang-an in China to the eastern gate of Kapilavastu in India is one hundred thousand leagues, so Chu-hung's criticism of *The Platform Sutra* for mistaking India for the Pure Land can be said to have a solid basis in fact."[46]

Now that's not even good rubbish. But even allowing (alas!) that the author's penchant for poking into old books is justified, I want him to tell me: What gazeteer or geography since the time of the Great Yü[47] ever stated that India is distant from China by ten evils and eight wrong practices? It's a great shame, really. Instead of wasting his time nosing through reference books, why didn't he just read *The Platform Sutra* with care and respect, and devote himself attentively to investigating Shakyamuni Buddha's true meaning in preaching about the Pure Land of Amida Buddha? If he had continued to contemplate that meaning, to ponder it this way and that way, coming and going, the time would have arrived when he would suddenly have broken through and grasped it. Then he would have had that "solid basis" he wants. He would be clapping his hands joyfully, howling with laughter—he couldn't have helped himself. And what, do you suppose, that great laughter would be about?

It is absurd for someone in Master Chu-hung's advanced state of spiritual myopia to be going around delivering wild judgments on the golden utterances of a genuine sage like the Sixth Patriarch. The same goes for the author of the *Kōkan*. Like Master Chu-hung, he spends his entire life living down inside a dark cave, inextricably tangled in a jungle of vines. They act like a midget sitting in a crowded theater. He tries to watch the play but is unable to see anything, so he jumps up and down and applauds when everyone else does. They also remind you of a troop of blind Persians who stumble upon a parchment leaf inscribed with Sanskrit letters. They wander off with it into the middle of nowhere, pool their knowledge and attempt to decipher the meaning of the text, but not having the faintest idea what it says, they fail to get even a single word right, and turn themselves into laughingstocks in the bargain.

Actually, such people should not even merit our attention, and yet because I am concerned about the harm they can do by misleading even a few sincere seekers, I find it necessary to lay down a few entangling vines of my own like this.

"The greatest care must be taken to keep such a work from beginning students," says Chu-hung's commentary. "If it does chance to fall into the hands of those who lack the capacity to understand it, it will turn them into wild demons of destruction. That would be deplorable."

My answer to the gross irresponsibility of such a statement is this: we must take the greatest care not to pass stupid, misinformed judgments on a work like *The Platform Sutra*. If people with unenlightened views judge such a work on the basis of their own ignorance, they will immediately transform themselves into wild demons of destruction. *That* is what would be deplorable.

To begin with, tathagatas appear in the world one after another for the sole purpose of opening up paths to buddha-wisdom so sentient beings can share their realization. That has always been their primary aim in manifesting themselves. Although the sutras and commentaries contain a variety of Dharma "gates"—abrupt and gradual teachings, verbal and preverbal teachings, exoteric and esoteric teachings, first and last teachings—in the end they all come down to one teaching and one teaching alone: the fundamental self-nature inherent in each and every person.

It is no different in Master Hui-neng's case. While *The Platform Sutra* containing his teaching has chapters devoted to his religious career, to his answers to questioners' doubts, to meditation and wisdom, to repentence, and so on, they are in the end none other than the one teaching of *kenshō* [seeing into true self-nature]. Wise sages for twenty-eight generations in India and six generations in China, as well as venerable Zen teachers of the Five Houses and Seven Schools who descended from them, have every one of them transmitted this Dharma of *kenshō* as they strove to lead people to awakening in Shakyamuni's place, devoting themselves single-mindedly to achieving the fundamental aim for which all buddhas appear in the world. None of them ever uttered one word about the Western Paradise, nor preached a single syllable about birth in the Pure Land. When the students who came after them began their study of the Way and took it upon themselves to read *The Platform Sutra*, none of them ever transformed into a wild demon. On the contrary, it deepened their attainment and enabled them to mature into great Dharma vessels. So please, Master Chu-hung, stop telling us about what you deplore.

It is because of misguided men like you that Nan-hai Tsung-pao of the Yüan dynasty wrote:

> *The Platform Sutra* is not mere words. It is the principle of Bodhidharma's "direct pointing" (at the mind) that has been transmitted from patriarch to patriarch. Thanks to it, great and venerable masters in the past like Nan-yüeh and Ch'ing-yüan cleared their minds; it cleared the minds of their disciples Ma-tsu and Shih-t'ou. The spread of the Zen school throughout the world today is also firmly rooted in this same principle of direct pointing. Indeed, is it possible that anyone in the future could clear his mind and see into his own nature without recourse to this same direct pointing?[48]

These words of Tsung-pao represent the accepted norm in Zen temples and monasteries everywhere. Yet there is Master Chu-hung ensconced in some remote temple, giving forth with those partisan hunches of his. The one is as different from the other as cloud from mud.

Since some people are naturally perceptive and some are not, and some have great ability while others have less, there is a correspondingly great variety in the teachings that buddhas impart to them. Buddhas work in the manner of a skilled physician. A physician does not set out to examine his patients with a single fixed medical prescription already in mind; since the ailments from which they suffer vary greatly, he must be able to prescribe a wide variety of remedies.

Take, for example, the desire for rebirth found among followers of the Pure Land school. Shakyamuni, the Great Physician King who relieves the suffering of sentient beings, in order to save Queen Vaidehi from the misery of a cruel imprisonment, converted her to firm belief in the Pure Land of her own intrinsic mind-nature by using good and skillful means that he devised for her particular situation. It was a specific remedy prescribed for the occasion and imparted to Queen Vaidehi alone.[49]

Men like Chu-hung, not having penetrated the truth of the Buddha's wonderful skillful means, cling mulishly to the deluded notion of a Pure Land and a buddha that exist separately, apart from the mind. They are incapable of truly grasping that there is no such thing as a buddha with his own buddha-land, that the village they see right in front of them and the village behind them and everywhere else—it is all buddha-land. There is no such thing as a buddha-body either. South and north, east and west, everywhere is the buddha-body in its entirety. When Chu-hung, being incapable of truly grasping such truths, heard a genuine Buddhist teaching such as the one that declared, "You are separated from the Western Paradise by the ten evils and eight false practices in yourself," he was appalled to find it did not agree with the conception of the Pure Land he had created in his own mind. He figured that if he roundly condemned it, he could keep others from hearing or reading about it.

If we let Chu-hung have his way and keep beginners from reading *The Platform Sutra* on the grounds that it is unsuitable for them, then *The Flower Garland Sutra*, and the *Lotus, Nirvana,* and other Mahayana sutras in which the Buddha reveals the substance of his enlightenment are not suitable for them either. I say this because the great master Hui-neng, having penetrated the profound and subtle principle of the buddha-mind, having broken decisively through the deep ground whence the ocean of Buddhist teaching finds its source, spoke with the same tongue, sang from the same mouth, as all the other buddhas.

Furthermore, a Chinese commentary on *The Flower Garland Sutra*, the *Hua-yen Ho-lun*, states that:

> aspirants belonging to the first rank recognize the Buddha's great power, observe his precepts and, by utilizing the power of the vow working in themselves, gain birth in his Pure Land. But that is not a real Pure Land, only a provisional manifestation of one. The reason aspirants seek it is because they have not seen into their own true nature, hence do not know that ignorance is in itself the fundamental wisdom of the tathagatas, and are thus still subject to the working of causation. This is the principle from which the preaching of a scripture such as *The Amida Sutra* is expounded."[50]

We may be sure if Chu-hung had seen this passage, he would have grabbed his brush and dashed off some lines about the *Hua-yen Ho-lun* being unfit for beginners. The *Hua-yen Ho-lun* is fortunate indeed to have avoided the blind-eyed gaze of the "Great Teacher of the Lotus Pond."[51] It saves us from having to listen to warnings about "giving it to people of small capacity," and "turning them into wild demons." Tsao-po Ta-shih (author of the *Ho-lun*), dwelling within the stillness of eternal samadhi, should be absolutely delighted at this stroke of good fortune.

Seen by the light of the true Dharma eye, all people—the old and the young, the high and the low, priests and laypeople, wise and otherwise—are endowed with the wonderful virtue of buddha-wisdom. It is present without any lack in all of them. Not one among them—or even half of one—is to be cast aside and rejected because he is a beginner.

Nonetheless, since students who are first setting out along the Way do not know what is beneficial to their practice and what is not, and can't distinguish immediate needs from less urgent ones, we refer to them for the time being as beginners. They read the sacred Buddhist writings and entrust themselves to the guidance of a good friend and teacher. Later, upon bringing the Great Matter to completion and fully maturing into true Dharma vessels, they will acquire a wonderful gift for expressing their attainment and, using that ability, will strive to impart the great Dharma-gift to others, holding buddha-wisdom up like a sun to illuminate the eternal darkness, keeping the vital pulse of that wisdom alive through the degenerate age of the latter day. It is these we can call true descendants of the buddhas, those whose debt of gratitude to their predecessors has been repaid in full.

But if they are compelled to practice the *nembutsu* along with all other students of whatever kind and capacity, on the grounds that they are beginners, we will have all the redoubtable members of the younger generation—those Bodhidharma praised as being "native born to the Mahayana in this land," people gifted with outstanding talent, who have it in them to become great Dharma pillars worthy to stand in the future with Te-shan, Lin-chi, Ma-tsu, and Shih-t'ou—traipsing along after half-dead old duffers, sitting in the shade next to the pond with listless old grannies, dropping their heads and closing their eyes in broad daylight and intoning endless choruses of *nembutsu*. If that happens, whose children will be found to carry on the vital pulse of buddha-wisdom? Who will become the cool, refreshing shade trees to provide refuge for people in the latter day? All the authentic customs and traditions of the Zen school will fall into the dust. The seeds of buddhahood will wither, die, and disappear forever.

I want these great and stalwart students of superior capacity to choose the right path. If, at a crucial time like this, the golden words in the Buddhist canon, all the Mahayana sutras that were compiled in the Pippali cave[52] for beginners to use in after ages, everything except the three Pure Land sutras, is relegated to the back shelves of the bookcase and left there untouched to end up as bug-fodder, buried in the bellies of bookworms, it will be no different from stacks of fake burial money piled forgotten in an old shrine deep in the mountains, of absolutely no use to anyone. It would be deplorable! Those people mentioned before—the ones *The Meditation Sutra* says are "destined for the highest rank of the highest rebirth in the Pure Land, suited to read the Mahayana sutras"—would cease to exist.

In the way that it slanderously rejects anything counter to its author's own notions, Chu-hung's commentary can be compared to the book-burning pit of the infamous Ch'in emperor.[53] The Ch'in emperor, deeply resentful when he found that his tyrannical policies were totally at odds with the ancient teachings in the Confucian writings, had the Confucian teachers buried alive and all their books consigned to the flames. Chu-hung has perpetrated a disaster of similar proportions.

The policies the three Wu emperors adopted to suppress Buddhism were undisguised.[54] Chu-hung worked to destroy the true teachings secretly. The former did it openly, the latter did it on the sly, yet the crime is one. However, Chu-hung is not really to blame for his transgressions. He did what he did because he had never encountered an authentic master to guide him and was thus unable to open the true Dharma eye that would have enabled him to see through into the secret depths. He did not possess the wonderful spiritual power that comes from *kenshō*.

Yet Chu-hung is given as "an example for good teachers past, present, and future." People praise him as "foremost among the great priests of the Zen, Teaching, and Precepts schools." They must be out of their minds!

The Zen forests of today will be found, upon inspection, to be thickly infested with a race of bonzes very similar to Chu-hung. They are everywhere, fastened with a grip of death to the "silent tranquillity" of their "withered-tree" sitting, which they imagine to be the true practice of the Buddha's Way. They don't take kindly to views that don't agree with their own convictions, so they regard the Buddha's sutras as they would a mortal enemy and forbid students to read them: they fear them as an evil spirit fears a sacred amulet. They are foolishly wedded to ordinary perception and experience, believing that to be Zen, and they take offense at anything that differs from their own ideas, so they view the records of the Zen patriarchs as they would a deadly adversary and refuse to allow their students near them: they avoid them as a lame hare avoids the hungry tiger.

With adherents of the Pure Land tradition shunning and disparaging the sacred scriptures of the buddhas and followers of Zen trying to discredit them with their slander, the danger to the Buddhist Way must be said to have reached a critical stage.

Don't get me wrong. I am not urging students to become masters of the classics and histories, to spend all their time exploring ancient

Chinese writings, or to lose themselves in the pleasures of poetry and letters; I am not telling them to compete against others and win fame for themselves by proving their superiority. They could attain an eloquence equal to that of the Great Purna, possess knowledge so great they surpassed Shariputra, but if they are lacking in the basic stuff of enlightenment, if they do not have the right eye of *kenshō*, false views, bred from arrogance, will inevitably find their way deep into their spiritual vitals, blasting the life from the seed of buddhahood, and saddling them with a one-way ticket to hell.

It is not like that with true followers of the Way. They must as an essential first step see their own original nature as clearly as if they are looking at the palm of their hand. When from time to time they read the scriptures that contain the words and teachings of the buddha-patriarchs, they will illuminate those ancient teachings with their own minds. They will visit genuine teachers for guidance. They will pledge with firm determination to work their way through the final koans of the patriarch teachers and, before they die, to produce from their forge a descendant—one person or at least half a person—as a way of repaying their deep debt of gratitude to the buddha-patriarchs. It is such people who are worthy to be called "the progeny of the house of Zen."

I respectfully submit to the "Great Teacher of the Lotus Pond": If you wish to plant yourself out in some hinterland where you can be free to finger your lotus-bead rosary, droop your head, drop your eyelids, and intone the *nembutsu* because you want to be born in the Land of Lotus Flowers, that is no business of mine. It is entirely up to you. But when you start gazing elsewhere with that myopic look in your eyes and decide to divert yourself by writing commentaries that pass belittling judgment on a great saint and matchless Dharma-transmitter like the Sixth Patriarch, then I must ask you to take the words you have written and shelve them away far out of sight, where no one will ever lay eyes on them. Why do I say that? I say it because the great Dragon King, who controls the clouds that sail in the heavens and the rains that fall over the earth, cannot be known or fathomed by a mud snail or a clam.

One of the worthy teachers of the past explained it thus:

> The "western quarter" refers to the original mind of sentient beings. "Passing beyond millions and millions of buddha-lands" [to

attain rebirth in the Pure Land] signifies sentient beings terminating the ten evil thoughts and abruptly transcending the ten stages of bodhisattvahood. "Amida," signifying immeasurable life, stands for the buddha-nature in sentient beings. "Kannon" and "Seishi," the bodhisattva attendants of Amida, represent the incomprehensible working of original self-nature. "Sentient being" is ignorance and the many thoughts, fears, discernments, and discriminations that result from it. "When life ends" refers to the time when discriminations and emotions cease to arise. "Cessation of intellection and discrimination" is the purifying of the original mind-ground, and indicates the Pure Land in the West.

It is to the west that sun, moon, and stars all return. In the same way, it is to the one universal mind that all the thoughts, fears, and discriminations of sentient beings return. It is thus one single mind, calm and undisturbed. And because Amida Buddha exists here, when you awaken to your self-nature the eighty-four thousand evil passions transform instantly into eighty-four thousand marvelous virtues. To the incomprehensible working that brings this about, we give the names Kannon, Seishi, and so on. The uneasy mind you have while you are in a state of illusion is called the defiled land. When you awaken and your mind is clear and free of defilement, that is called the Pure Land.[55]

Hence in *The Essay on the Dharma Pulse* Bodhidharma says that "the nembutsu practiced by Buddhist saints in the past was not directed toward an external buddha; their nembutsu practice was oriented solely toward the internal buddha in their own minds. . . . If you want to discover buddha, you must first of all see into your own true nature. Unless you have seen into your own nature, what good can come from doing nembutsu or reciting sutras?"[56]

4

THE DIFFICULTY OF REPAYING
THE DEBT TO THE BUDDHAS AND
THE PATRIARCHS

Buddha means "one who is awakened."[1] Once you have awakened, your own mind itself is buddha. By seeking outside yourself for a buddha invested with form, you set yourself forward as a foolish, misguided man. It is like a person who wants to catch a fish. He must start by looking in the water, because fish live in water and are not found apart from it. If a person wants to find buddha, he must look into his own mind, because it is there, and nowhere else, that buddha exists.

Question: "In that case, what can I do to become awakened to my own mind?"

What is that which asks such a question? Is it your mind? Is it your original nature? Is it some kind of spirit or demon? Is it inside you? Outside you? Is it somewhere intermediate? Is it blue, yellow, red, or white?

It is something you must investigate and clarify for yourself. You must investigate it whether you are standing or sitting, speaking or silent, when you are eating your rice or drinking your tea. You must keep at it with total, single-minded devotion. And never, whatever you do, look in sutras or in commentaries for an answer, or seek it in the words you hear a teacher speak.

When all the effort you can muster has been exhausted and you have reached a total impasse, and you are like the cat at the rathole, like the mother hen warming her egg, it will suddenly come and you will break free. The phoenix will get through the golden net. The crane will fly clear of the cage.

But even if no breakthrough occurs until your dying day and you spend twenty or thirty years in vain without ever seeing into your true nature, I want your solemn pledge that you will never turn for spiritual support to those tales that you hear the down-and-out old men and washed-out old women peddling everywhere today. If you do, they will stick to your hide, they will cling to your bones, you will never be free of them. And as for your chances with the patriarchs' difficult-to-pass koans, the less said about them the better, because they will be totally beyond your grasp.

Hence a priest of former times, Kao-feng Yüan-miao, said, "A person who commits himself to the practice of Zen must be equipped with three essentials. A great root of faith. A great ball of doubt. A great tenacity of purpose. Lacking any one of them, he is like a tripod with only two legs."[2]

By "great root of faith" is meant the belief that each and every person has an essential self-nature he can see into, and the belief in a principle by which this self-nature can be fully penetrated. Even though you attain this belief, you cannot break through and penetrate to total awakening unless feelings of fundamental doubt arise as you work on the difficult-to-pass [*nantō*] koans. And even if these doubts build up, and crystallize, and you yourself become a "great doubting mass," you will be unable to break that doubting mass apart unless you constantly bore into those koans with a great, burning tenacity of purpose.

Thus it is said that it takes three long kalpas for lazy and inattentive sentient beings to attain nirvana, while for the fearless and stout-hearted, buddhahood comes in a single instant of thought. What you must do is to concentrate single-mindedly on bringing all your native potential into play. The practice of Zen is like making a fire by friction. The essential thing as you rub wood against stone is to apply continuous, all-out effort. If you stop when you see the first sign of smoke, you will never get even a flicker of fire, even though you keep rubbing away for two or three kalpas.

Only a few hundred yards from here is a beach. Suppose someone is bothered because he has never tasted sea water and decides to sample some. He sets out in the direction of the beach, but before he has gone a hundred paces he stops and comes back. He starts out again, but this time he returns after he has taken only ten steps. He will never get to know the taste of sea water that way, will he? But if he keeps going straight ahead without turning back, even if he lives far inland in a landlocked province such as Shinano, Kai, Hida, or Mino, he will eventually reach the sea. By dipping his finger in the water and tasting it, he will know instantly the taste of sea water the world over, because it is of course the same everywhere, in India, China, the southern sea or the northern sea.

Those Dharma patricians who explore the secret depths are like this too. They go straight forward, boring into their own minds with unbroken effort, never letting up or retreating. Then the breakthrough suddenly comes, and with that they penetrate their own nature, the nature of others, the nature of sentient beings, the nature of the evil passions and of enlightenment, the nature of the buddhanature, the god nature, the bodhisattva nature, the sentient-being nature, the nonsentient-being nature, the craving-ghost nature, the contentious-spirit nature, the beast nature—they are all of them seen in a single instant of thought. The great matter of their religious quest is completely and utterly resolved. There is nothing left. They are free of birth and death. What a thrilling moment it is!

It is with great respect and deep reverence that I urge all you superior seekers who investigate the secret depths to be as earnest in penetrating and clarifying the self as you would be putting out a fire on top of your head; to be as assiduous in boring through your doubt as you would be seeking a lost article of incalculable worth; to be as hostile toward the teachings left by the Buddha-patriarchs as you would be toward a person who had just slain both your parents. Anyone belonging to the school of Zen who does not engage in the doubting and introspection of koans must be considered a deadbeat rascal of the lowest type, a person who would throw away the greatest asset he has. Hence Kao-feng said, "At the bottom of great doubt lies great enlightenment. . . . A full measure of doubt will become a full measure of enlightenment."

Don't think the commitments and pressing duties of secular life leave you no time to go about forming a ball of doubt. Don't think your mind is so crowded with confused thoughts you would be incapable of devoting yourself single-mindedly to Zen practice. Suppose a man was in a busy marketplace, pushing his way down a narrow street in a dense crowd, and some gold coins happened to drop out of his pocket into the dirt. Do you imagine he would just leave them there, forget about them, and continue on his way because of where he was? Do you think someone would leave the gold pieces behind because he was in a congested place or because the coins were lying in the dirt? Of course not. He would be down there pushing and shoving as much as he had to, frantically turning everything upside down, with tears in his eyes. His mind wouldn't rest until he had recovered them. Yet what are a few pieces of gold set against the priceless jewel found in the headdresses of kings, that way of inconceivable being that exists within your own mind?[3] Could a jewel of such worth be attained easily, without effort?

There once was a denizen of the Eastern Sea, Redfin Carp by name, who was endowed with an indomitable spirit and an upright character. Redfin Carp was a figure of immense stature among his fellow fish. He was constantly bemoaning the fate of his comrades. "How many untold millions of my brethren proudly dwell in the vast ocean deeps. They entrust themselves to its boundless silver waves, glide up and down among the swells, and sport in the seaweed and kelp. Yet countless of them are taken by baited hooks and caught in nets. They wind up on chopping blocks, where they are sliced and cooked to fill the bellies of those in the human world. Their bones are cast away and left to mingle in the dust and mire. Their heads are thrown to the stray dogs. Some are dried or salted for inland markets. Exposed in stalls and shopfronts for all to see. Not a single one finishes out his natural span. How sad is the life of a fish!"

Amid these sad musings there was a great welling of spirit in Redfin Carp's breast. He pledged a solemn vow. "I shall swim beyond the Dragon Gates.[4] I shall brave the perilous bolts of fire and lightning. I shall transcend the estate of ordinary fish and achieve a place among the order of sacred dragons. I shall rid myself forever of the terrible suffering to which my race is heir, expunge every trace of our shame and humiliation."

Waiting until the third day of the third month, when the peach blossoms are in flower and the river is full, he made his way to the entrance of the Yü Barrier. Then, with a flick of his tail, Redfin Carp swam forth.

You men have never laid eyes on the awesome torrent of water that rolls through the Dragon Gates. It falls all the way from the summits of the far-off Kunlun Range with tremendous force. There are wild, thousand-foot waves that rush down through gorges towering to dizzying heights on either side, carrying away whole hillsides as they go. Angry bolts of thunder beat down with a deafening roar. Moaning whirlwinds whip up poisonous mists and funnels of noisome vapor spitting flashing forks of lightning. The mountain spirits are stunned into senselessness; the river spirits turn limp with fright. Just a drop of this water will shatter the carapace of the giant tortoise, it will break the bones of the giant whale.

It was into this maelstrom that Redfin Carp, his splendid golden-red scales girded to the full, his steely teeth thrumming like drums, made a direct all-out assault. Ah! Golden Carp! Golden Carp! You might have led an ordinary life out in the boundless ocean. It teems with lesser fish. You would not have gone hungry. Then why? What made you embark on this wild and bitter struggle? What was waiting for you up beyond the Barrier?

Suddenly, after being seared by cliff-shattering bolts of lightning, after being battered by heaven-scorching blasts of thunderfire, his scaly armor burnt from head to tail, his fins singed through, Redfin Carp perished into the Great Death and rose again as a divine dragon—a supreme lord of the waters. Now, with the thunder god at his head and the fire god at his rear, flanked right and left by the gods of rain and wind, he moves abroad with the clouds in one hand and the mists in the other, bringing new life to the tender young shoots withering in long-parched desert lands, keeping the true Dharma safe amid the defilements of the degenerate world.

Had he been content to pass his life like a lame turtle or blind tortoise, feeding on winkles and tiny shrimps, not even all the effort Vasuki, Manasvi, and the other Dragon Kings might muster on his behalf could have done him any good. He could never have achieved the great success that he did.

What do I mean by "blind tortoise"? One of the current crop of sightless, irresponsible bungler-priests who regard the koan as nonessential, and the Zen interview (*sanzen*) as the master's expedient means. While even such men are not totally devoid of understanding, they are clearly standing outside the gates, whence they peer fecklessly in, mouthing words like, "Self-nature is naturally pure, the mind-source is deep as an ocean. There is no samsaric existence to cast aside, there is no nirvana to be sought. It is a sheer and profound stillness, a transparent mass of boundless emptiness. It is here that is found the great treasure inherent in all people. How could anything be lacking?"

Ah, how plausible it sounds! All too plausible. Unfortunately, the words they speak do not possess even a shred of strength in practical application. These people are like snails. The moment anything approaches, they draw in their horns and come to a standstill. They are like lame turtles; they pull in their legs, heads, and tails at the slightest contact and hide inside their shells. How can any spiritual energy emerge from such an attitude? If they chance to encounter an authentic monk and are subjected to a sharp verbal attack, they react like Master Yang's pet stork who, when the time came to perform, couldn't even move his neck.[5] There's no difference between them and the fish who lie helpless on the chopping block, dying ten thousand deaths in their one life, their fate—whether they are to be sliced and served up raw, or carved into fillets and roasted over hot coals— entirely in the hands of others. And throughout their ordeal they haven't even the strength to cry out. Can people of this kind be true descendants of the great Bodhidharma? They assure you that there is "nothing lacking." But are they happy? Are their minds free of care?

Genuine monks who negotiated the Way in the past flung themselves and everything they owned into their masters' white-hot forges without a thought for their own lives or well-being. Once their minds were turned to the Way, they too, like Redfin Carp, gathered all their strength and courage and strove until they broke beyond the Dragon Gates. Thereafter, in whatever situation, under whatever circumstance, they functioned with total self-dependence and perfect, unattached freedom. What intense joy and gratification they must have enjoyed. It is these people you must emulate, not the stork. Not those turtles and snails.

And what are "sacred dragons"? Those vital patriarchs of the past, absolutely genuine and true, who committed themselves solely and single-mindedly to the authentic practice of Zen. Ah, you are human beings, aren't you? If you let yourselves be outdone by a fish, you might just as well be dead already!

There is yet another type of obstructive demon you often run up against, the ones who teach their followers:

> If you want to attain mastery in the Buddha Way you must, to begin with, empty your mind of birth and death. Both samsara and nirvana exist because the mind gives rise to them. The same for the heavens and hells; not one of them exists unless the mind produces them. Hence there is one and one thing only for you to do: make your minds completely empty.

Falling right into step, students set out to empty their minds, make them utter blanks. The trouble is, though they try everything they know, emptying this way, emptying that way, working away at it for months, even years, they find it is like trying to sweep mist away by flailing at it with a pole, or trying to stem the flow of a river by blocking it with outstretched arms. The only result is greater confusion.

Suppose, for example, that a wealthy man mistakenly hires a master thief of the greatest skill and cunning to guard his house. After watching his granaries, treasures, and the rest of his fortune dwindle by the day, he orders the thief to seize several suspicious servants and to interrogate them around the clock until they confess. Family members are worried sick. Relations between husband and wife are severely strained. Yet their fortune goes on mysteriously shrinking. And it all happens because of the mistake the man had made in the beginning, in employing and placing his complete trust in a thief.

The lesson to be learned from this is that the very attempts to banish birth and death from your mind are, in themselves, a sure sign that birth and death is in full progress.

In the *Shurangama Sutra* the Buddha says, "From the beginningless past right up to your present existence you have mistakenly regarded a thief as your own son and your changeless original nature has thus been lost to you. Because of that you have been transmigrating through the cycle of birth and death." This is explained in a commentary on the sutra:

> The word *thief* is used to describe the manner in which you are deprived of the merits of the Dharma resource. Being deluded and thus unaware of this situation, you mistakenly regard this *thief* as something true and changeless and entrust your most valuable possessions to him in the belief he is your legitimate heir. Instead you bring about your own downfall, and reduce yourself to the wretchedness and poverty of being forever separated from the Dharma treasure.[6]

If you really want to empty your mind of birth and death, what you should do is tackle one of the totally impregnable, hard-to-pass koans. When you merge suddenly with the basic root of life and everything ceases to exist, you will know for the first time the profound meaning contained in the great master Yung-chia's words, "Do not brush illusions away, do not seek the truth of enlightenment."[7]

Zen master Ta-hui said, "At the present time, the Evil One's influence is strong and the Dharma is weak. The great majority of people regard 'reverting to tranquility and living within it' as the ultimate attainment."[8] He also said:

> A race of sham Zennists has appeared in recent years who consider sitting with dropped eyelids and closed mouths and letting illusory thoughts spin through their minds to be the attainment of a marvelous state that surpasses human understanding. They regard it as the realm of primal buddhahood "existing prior to the timeless beginning." And if they do open their mouths and utter so much as a syllable, they immediately tell you that they have fallen out of that marvelous realm. They believe this to be the most fundamental state it is possible to attain. Satori is a mere side issue—"a twig or branch." Such people are completely mistaken from the time they take their first step along the Way.[9]

These people who ally themselves with the devil are present in great numbers today as well. To them I say, "Never mind for now about what you consider 'nonessential side issues.' Tell me about your own fundamental matter, the one you hide away treasuring so zeal-ously. What is it like? Is it a piece of solid emptiness fixed firmly in the ground somewhere—like a post for tethering mules and horses? Or maybe it's a deep hole filled with a sheer black silence? Whatever it is, it makes my flesh creep."

It is also a good example of what is called falling into fixed views. It deceives a great many of the foolish and ignorant of the world. It's an ancient dwelling place of evil spirits, an old badger's den, a pitfall that traps people and buries them alive. Although you kept treasuring and defending it till the end of time, it would still be just a fragment of an old coffin. It also goes by the name of "dark cave of the eighth Alaya consciousness."[10] The ancients suffered through a great many hardships as they wandered in arduous pursuit of the truth. It was all for the sole purpose of getting themselves free of just such stinking old nests as these.

Once a person is able to achieve true single-mindedness in his prac-tice and smash apart the old nest of Alaya consciousness into which he has settled, the Great Perfect Mirror Wisdom immediately ap-pears, the other three great Wisdoms start to function, and the all-embracing Fivefold Eye opens wide.

If, on the other hand, he allows himself to be seduced by these latter-day devils into hunkering down inside an old nest and making himself at home there, turning it into a private treasure chamber and spending all his time dusting and polishing it, sweeping and brushing it clean, what can he hope to achieve? Absolutely nothing. Basically, it is a piece of the eighth consciousness, the same eighth consciousness that enters the womb of a donkey and enters the belly of a horse. So I urgently exhort you to do everything you can, strive with all your strength, to strike down into that dark cave and smash your way open into freedom.

On that day long ago when the World-honored One attained his great awakening and clothed himself in the precious celestial robe to expound the true heart of the extensive *Flower Garland Sutra*, he preached for three whole weeks to an audience that listened, without comprehending, as though they were deaf and dumb.[11] Thereupon, in order to make salvation accessible to people of mediocre and infe-rior capacity, he erected a temporary resting place for them to use on the way to ultimate attainment. He called this provisional abode a "phantom dwelling." After that, Shakyamuni did his best to destroy this abode by preaching against it from within the Buddhist order; Layman Vimalakirti attempted to do the same by inveighing against it from without. They even likened those who attach to it, the adherents of the Two Vehicles [those who are content just to listen to the Buddha's teaching and those who remain satisfied to enjoy their own private realization] to "suppurating old polecats." But in the end they were between them unable to eradicate that dwelling place at its source in the Alaya consciousness.

Gradually, the foster children spawned by adherents of the Two Vehicles multiplied. Slowly and imperceptibly they spread throughout India and the western regions. In time, even China was filled with them. There, venerable masters like Tz'u-ming, Hsin-ching, Yüan-wu, and Ta-hui set their jaws, clenched their teeth, and strove valiantly to root them out, but even for them it was like trying to drive off a wily old rat by clapping your hands. He disappears over here, but he reappears over there, always lurking somewhere, furtively disparaging the true, untransmittable style of the patriarchal teachers. How lamentable!

In Japan, during the Jōkyū (1219–1221), Katei (1235–1237), Karyaku (1326–1328), and Kembu (1334–1335) eras, twenty-four wise Zen sages entrusted their lives to the perilous whale-backed eastern seas, cast themselves bodily into the tiger's den, in order to transmit the difficult-to-believe methods of our authentic traditions. They fervently desired to fix the sun of wisdom permanently in the highest branches of the Divine Mulberry; to hang a precious Dharma lamp that would illuminate forever the dark hamlets of the Dragonfly Provinces.[12] How could any of them have foreseen that their transmission would be slandered and maligned by these quietistic pseudo-Zennists and that in less than three hundred years the Zen they had transmitted would be lying in the dust? Would have no more life in it than last night's ashes? Nothing could be more distressing than to witness the wasting away of the true Dharma in a degenerate age like this.

On the other hand, if a single person of superior capacity commits himself to the authentic pursuit of the Way and through sustained effort under the guidance of a true teacher fills with the power of sheer single-mindedness, then his normal processes of thought, perception, consciousness, and emotion will cease, he will reach the limits of words and reason. He will resemble an utter fool, as everything, including his erstwhile determination to pursue the Way, disappears and his breath itself hangs almost suspended. At that point, what a pity that a Buddhist teacher, one who is supposed to act as his "great and good friend," should be unaware that this is the occasion when the tortoise shell is about to crack, the phoenix about to break free of its egg; should not know that these are all favorable signs seen in those poised on the threshold of enlightenment, should be stirred by grandmotherly kindness and immediately give in to tender, effeminate feelings of compassion for the student and begin straight off explaining to him the reason for this and the principle for that, drawing him down into the abode of delusory surmise, pushing him over into the cave of intellectual understanding, and then taking a phony winter melon seal and certifying his enlightenment with the pronouncement, "You are like this. I am like this too. Preserve it carefully."[13] Ah! Ah! It's up to them if they want to preserve it. The trouble is, they are still as far from the patriarchal groves as earth is from heaven. What are to all appearances acts of kindness on the part of a teacher helping a student are, in fact, doings that will bring about his doom. For his part, the student, nodding with satisfaction and without an inkling of the mortal injury he has incurred, prances and frisks about wagging his tail, proud in the knowledge: "Now I have grasped the secret of Bodhidharma's coming from the West."

How are such students to know they haven't made it past any of the patriarchs' Barriers? That the thorny forests of Zen are much, much deeper than they can even conceive? What a terrible shame for people of marvelous gifts, unexcelled capacity, who have it in them to become great beams and pillars of the house of Zen, to succumb to these corrupting winds and to spend the rest of their lives in a half-waking, half-drunk state, no different from the dull and witless type of people who never get around to doubting their way through anything! Is it any wonder that the groves of Zen are so barren of real men? A person who attachs to half-truths of this kind believing them to be essential and ultimate will probably not even know that he has fallen into the unfortunate category of "withered buds and shriveled seeds."

Long ago, when Zen master Nan-yüeh sat in front of Ma-tsu's

hermitage and began polishing a tile, he did so because of his desire to make Ma-tsu grasp his true meaning. When teachers of the past left phrases behind them, difficult-to-penetrate koans that would strip students' minds of their chronic inclination to attach to things, they did it because they wanted to kick over that comfortable old nesting place in the Alaya consciousness. Hence a master of the past said, "I made the mistake of burrowing into an old jackal hole for over thirty years myself; it's no mystery to me why so many students do the same."[14]

There's no doubt about it, the practice of Zen is a formidable undertaking.

In his later years, the Zen master Fa-yen enjoyed strolling the south corridor of his temple on Mount Wu-tsu. One day he saw a visiting monk pass by reading a book. He took it from him and, glancing through it, came to a passage that caught his attention:

> Most Zen students today are able to reach a state of serenity in which their minds and bodies are no longer troubled by afflicting passions, and their attachment to past and future is cut away so that each instant contains all time. There they stop and abide contently like censers lying useless and forgotten in an ancient cemetery, cold and lifeless with nothing to break the silence but the sobbing of the dead spirits. Assuming this to be the ultimate Zen has to offer them, they are unaware that what they consider an unsurpassed realm is in fact obstructing their true self so that true knowing and seeing cannot appear and the radiant light of extraordinary spiritual power (*jinzū*) cannot shine free."[15]

Fa-yen closed the book and, raising his arms in a gesture of self-reproach for his ignorance, exclaimed, "Extraordinary! Here is a true teacher! How well he expresses the essence of the Zen school!"

He hurried to the quarters of his student Yüan-wu, who was serving as head monk, calling out to him, "It's extraordinary! Really and truly extraordinary!" He placed the book in Yüan-wu's hands and had him read it too. Then Dharma father and Dharma son, unable to contain their joy, acclaimed the author with the most enthusiastic praise.

When Ta-hui went to study under Zen master Yüan-wu for the first time, he had already decided on a course of action. "By the end of the ninety-day summer retreat," he declared to himself, "if Yüan-wu has affirmed my understanding like all the other teachers I've been to, I'm going to write a treatise debunking Zen."

Ta-hui, did you really think Yüan-wu wouldn't be able to see through the fundamental matter you secretly treasured? If you had persisted in clinging to it like that, revering it and cherishing it for the rest of your life, how could the great "Reviler of Heaven" ever have emerged?

Fortunately, however, a poisonous breeze blowing from the south snuffed Ta-hui's life out at its roots, cutting away past and future.[16] When it happened, his teacher Yüan-wu said, "What you've accomplished is not easy. But you've merely finished killing your self. You're not capable of coming back to life and raising doubts about the words and phrases of the ancients. Your ailment is a serious one. You know the saying, 'Release your hold on the edge of the precipice. Die, and then be reborn'? You must believe in those words."

Later, upon hearing Yüan-wu say, "What happens when the tree falls and the wisteria withers? The same thing happens." Ta-hui suddenly achieved great enlightenment. When Yüan-wu tested him with several koans, he passed them easily.[17]

Ta-hui rose to become abbot of the Ching-shan monastery, the most important in the land, with a thousand resident monks. As he supervised this sterling collection of dragons and elephants he was like a hungry eagle gazing down on a covey of rabbits. We should feel honored to have a man of such profound attainment among the teachers of our school. Yet, as we have seen, there are some who consider such attainment unimportant—a nonessential "side issue." What they themselves regard as essential, and secretly cherish, is so worthless that even if you set it out together with a million pieces of gold, you would find no takers.

Yüan-wu said,

> After the ancients had once achieved awakening, they went off and lived in thatched huts or caves, boiling wild vegetable roots in broken-legged pots to sustain them. They weren't interested in making names for themselves or in rising to positions of power. Being perfectly free from all ties whatever, they left turning words for their descendants because they wanted to repay their profound debt to the Buddha-patriarchs.[18]

The priest Wan-an Tao-yen wrote a verse comment on the kōan Nan-ch'üan on the Mountain:

> Lying on a pillow of coral, his eyes filled with tears—
> Partly because he likes you, partly because he resents you.

When these lines came to Ta-hui's notice, he immediately ordered his attendant to take down the practice schedules (giving his monks a day of rest), saying, "With this single turning word Wan-an has amply requited his debt to the buddhas."[19]

Most priests furnish their altars with lamps and incense holders; they set out offerings of tea, flowers and sweets; they prostrate themselves before it over and over, and perform various other religious practices around the clock; some even inflict burns on their fingers, arms, and bodies. But none of that repays even a tenth of the debt they owe the buddhas. How, then, is it possible for a single couplet from an old poem, cutting away complicating entanglements, to immediately repay that debt—and repay it in full? This question is by no means an idle or trivial one. Ta-hui was the Dragon Gate of his age, a towering shade tree who provided shelter for over seventeen hundred students. Do you suppose a man of his stature would utter such words frivolously?

The priest Pa-ling had three turning words.[20] His teacher, the great Zen master Yün-men, told his disciples, "When I die, hold no funeral observances of any kind. Instead, I want each of you to take up these three turning words."

Now do you really believe that the reason a great patriarch such as Yün-men urged students to engage in what these people call "nonessentials" was simply because he happened to prefer them over funeral offerings of flowers, sweets, and rare foods?

Yüan-wu declared: If one of my monks came to me and said, "If there is essentially no moving forward to satori and no moving backward to the everyday world, what's the use of practicing Zen?" I'd just tell them, "I see you're down inside that pitchdark hole living with the other dead souls."[21] What a pitiful sight!

Yüan-wu said:

> Many people like to cite the sayings of the Buddhist sages or a phrase from the sutras such as "ordinary speech, subtle speech—it

all comes from the same ultimate source," persuaded that they really understand the meaning. If any of you here is operating under such an assumption, he'd be well advised to give up Zen altogether. He can devote his life to scholarship and become a celebrated exegete.

Nowadays you often hear people say, "There's essentially no such thing as satori. The gate or teaching of satori was established as a way of making this fact known to people." If that's the way you think, you're like a flea attached to the body of a lion, sustaining itself by drinking its life blood. Don't you know what the ancient worthy said: "If the source is not deep, the stream will not be long; if the wisdom is not great, the discernment will not be far-reaching"? If the Buddha's Dharma was a teaching that had been created or fabricated as they say, how could it have survived to the present day?

Ch'ang-sha Ching-ts'en sent a monk to the priest Tung-ssu Ju-huí, who was, like his teacher Nan-ch'üan, a disciple of Ma-tsu. The monk asked Ju-huí, "What was it like after you met Nan-ch'üan?" Ju-huí was silent.

"What was it like before you met Nan-ch'üan?" he asked. "No different from after I met him," said Ju-huí. The monk returned to Ch'ang-sha and gave him Ju-huí's response. Ch'ang-sha expressed his own thoughts in a verse:

> Perched motionless at the tip of a hundred-foot pole
> The man has attainment, but he hasn't made it real.
> He must advance one more step beyond the tip,
> Reveal his whole body in the ten directions.

Afterward, San-sheng Hui-jan sent a senior monk named Hsui to ask Ch'ang-sha some questions. "When Nan-ch'üan passed away, where did he go?" said Hsui.[22] "When Shih-t'ou was just a young monk, he visited the Sixth Patriarch," said Ch'ang-sha.

"I'm not asking about when Shih-t'ou was a young monk," replied Hsui. "I want to know where Nan-ch'üan went when he died." "Investigate him thoroughly," said Ch'ang-sha.[23]

"You're like a noble old pine tree towering thousands of feet in the winter sky," said Hsui. "You're not like a bamboo shoot springing straight up through the rocks." Ch'ang-sha was silent. "Thank you for your answers," said Hsui. Ch'ang-sha was still silent.

Hsui returned to San-sheng and told him about his meeting with Ch'ang-sha. "If that's the way Ch'ang-sha is," said San-sheng, "he's a good seven steps ahead of Lin-chi."

Now both Lin-chi and Ch'ang-sha are beyond question genuine dragons of the buddha ocean. They are the celestial phoenix and fabulous unicorn that frequent the Zen gardens of the patriarchs. There is no one comparable to them. Having far transcended all forms and appearances, they move slowly or move quickly in response to changing conditions, like huge masses of blazing fire, like iron stakes burning at white heat. Neither gods nor demons can perceive their traces; neither devils nor non-Buddhists can perceive their activity. Who could conceive their limits? Who could discern any difference between them?

Yet when San-sheng, who was himself a direct Dharma heir of Lin-chi, heard what Ch'ang-sha had said, he praised him as being superior to his own teacher! How can words be so awesomely difficult? You must understand, however, that contained within what is to you a mass of entangling verbal complications there is a small but wondrous something that is able to work miracles.

When Zen master Shih-shuang passed away and the brotherhood asked the head monk to succeed him as abbot, Zen master Chiu-feng Tao-ch'ien, who had previously served as the master's attendant, came and addressed them. He posed a question to the head monk, "The master often told us to 'cease all activity,' to 'do nothing whatever,' to 'become so cold and lifeless the spirits of the dead will come sighing around you,' to 'become a bolt of fine white silk,' to 'become dead ashes inside a censer in a forgotten old graveyard,' to 'become so that this very instant is ten thousand years.'

"What is the meaning of these instructions? If you show that you grasp them, you are the next abbot. If you show that you do not, you aren't the man for the job."

"His words," said the head monk, "refer to the essential oneness of all things." "You have failed to understand the master's meaning," said Chiu-feng.

"Get some incense ready," replied the head monk. "If I have ter-

minated my life by the time that incense burns down, it will mean I
grasped the master's meaning. If I am still living, it will mean I did
not."

Chiu-feng lit a stick of incense and, before it had burned down,
the head monk had ceased breathing. Patting the lifeless man on the
back, Chiu-feng said, "Other monks have died while seated; some of
them have died while standing. But you proved just now that you
could not have seen the master's meaning even in your dreams."

Often those who approach the end of their lives having devoted
themselves single-mindedly to the practice of the Way will regard the
solitude of their final hours, sitting in the light of a solitary lamp, as
the last great and difficult barrier of their religious quest, and as the
smoke from the incense burns down, they move quietly and calmly
into death, without ever having uttered an authentic Zen phrase of
any kind. It is they whom Chiu-feng is patting on the back when he
says, "You haven't grasped your late master's meaning." You should
reflect deeply on those words.

Once Zen master Yün-chü of Hung-chou had an attendant take a
pair of trousers to a monk who was living by himself in a grass hut.
The monk refused the trousers. He explained that "he already had
the pair he was born with." When Yün-chü was informed of the
monk's reply, he sent the attendant back to ask the question, "What
did you wear prior to your birth?" The monk could give no answer.
Later, when the monk died and his body was cremated, relics were
found among his ashes.[24] When these were shown to Yün-chü, he
said, "I'd much rather have had one phrase from him in response to
the question I asked when he was alive than ten bushels of relics from
a dead man."

The relics that are sometimes found among the ashes of virtuous
priests are said to be produced as a natural result of the great merit
they achieved in previous lives through meditation and wisdom.
Whenever a relic is discovered after a cremation, even if it is only the
size of a grain of millet or a mustard seed, crowds of people—men
and women, young and old, priests and laity—rush to see it. They
crowd around to marvel at it and worship it with expressions of deep
veneration. Yet Yün-chü declares that even ten bushels of such relics
would not be worth a single phrase uttered while the monk was alive.

What is this "one phrase" that it could be even more esteemed than a genuine Buddhist relic that everyone venerates so deeply? This question baffled me for a long time.

After the priest P'o-an Tsu-hsien had retired to the Tzu-fu-yüan Temple, he was invited to the monastery at Mount Ching by the abbot Meng-an Yüan-ts'ung, who appointed him to the post of head monk. Among the brotherhood at the monastery was a man of penetrating insight known as senior monk Pao. He always came when the abbot or head monk was receiving students, and by seizing the slightest opening and turning aside their thrusts with a sudden lightning attack, he invariably got the best of them.

One day, Pao came in while P'o-an was in his chambers receiving students. P'o-an was quoting a passage from *The Treatise of the Precious Treasury*, "Within heaven and earth, in the midst of the universe, there is here . . ."[25] Pao was about to say something, but before he did, P'o-an promptly slapped him and drove him out of the room.

Actually, Pao had intended to interject a comment the moment P'o-an had finished the quotation, but P'o-an had anticipated him. Pao was convinced that P'o-an was deliberately out to humiliate him, and after he left P'o-an's room he returned to his place in the meditation hall, sat down, and expired. When his body was cremated, villagers from the neighboring areas found some relics among his ashes. They took them and presented them to P'o-an. P'o-an held them up and said, "Senior Monk Pao, even if ten bushels of these had turned up among your ashes, I'd still set them aside. I just wanted that one turning word while you were alive!" With that, he dashed the relics against the ground. They turned out to be nothing but tiny bits of pus and blood.

An ancient worthy wrote,

> Of the seventeen hundred eminent masters included in *The Records of the Lamp*, relics were found among the ashes of only fourteen; they were recovered from only a handful of the eighty priests mentioned in *The Biographies of Monks from the Groves of Zen*. More importantly, we in our school regard only two things as essential: thorough attainment of self-realization and thorough mastery in instructing others. That means being armed with the fangs and

claws that spur students onward, dissolving their attachments and breaking their chains. Buddhists also call this "transmitting the Dharma, ferrying people to the other shore." Everything else is unimportant.[26]

The teachers of our Zen school have in their possession moves and maneuvers that are hard to believe, hard to understand, hard to penetrate, and hard to realize. They can take someone whose mind seems dead, devoid of consciousness, and transform him into a bright-eyed monk of awesome vitality. These methods we call the fangs and claws of the Dharma cave. It is like when an old tiger gives a long, blood-curdling roar and emerges from the forest; he throws such mortal fear into the rabbits, foxes, badgers, and their kind that they wobble around helplessly on rubbery knees, their livers petrified, their eyes fixed in glassy stares, piddling and shitting involuntarily. Why do they react that way? Because the tiger is armed with claws of steel and a set of shining golden fangs like a forest of razor-sharp swords. Without those weapons, tigers would be no different from other animals.

Hence these words by a Zen master of the past: "In the first year of the Kien-chung era (1101), I obtained at the quarters of a now-deceased friend a copy of Zen master Tung-shan Shou-ch'u's recorded sayings, compiled by his disciple Fu-yen Liang-ya. It contained words and phrases of great subtlety and profundity—the veritable claws and fangs of the Dharma cave."[27]

At the start of the Chien-tao era (1165–1174), when Hsia-tao Hui-yüan was abbot at the Kuo-ch'ing-ssu Temple, he happened to see a verse tribute that Huo-an Shih-t'i had dedicated to an image of the Bodhisattva Kannon.

> He doesn't stay settled within his primal being,
> And brings confusion to people the world over;
> Gazing up at him, worshipping him with reverence,
> They all have eyes, yet still they cannot see him.
> The natural beauties of Ch'ang-an are timeless,
> Why must people blindly grope along its walls?

Hsia-tao was beside himself with joy. "I had no idea there was someone of such ability among Master Shui-an's followers," he exclaimed. He had a search made and finally located Huo-an at the Chiang-hsin-ssu Temple. There, in the presence of a large gathering of people, he begged Huo-an to come and serve as his head monk.[28]

Often I hear people say how hard it is to judge others correctly. It was difficult even for the sages of olden times. Yet here is Master Hsia-tao, praising a man after reading only a few lines of verse he had written, then asking him to become head monk of his temple! Could it really have been as easy as that? Perhaps Hsia-tao was acting with undue haste. Or, perhaps there really is something in those lines of verse. These are questions that deserve our closest scrutiny.

Zen master Shui-an Shih-i of Ching-tz'u-yüan Temple, speaking to students in his chambers, said, "The western barbarian has no beard." One of the monks went to Huo-an Shih-t'i and told him what Shui-an had said. "A starving dog will eat cotton wool," declared Huo-an, "even if it's rotten."

The monk withdrew, then went back and reported Huo-an's words to Shui-an. "The man who uttered that is capable of teaching an assembly of five hundred monks," said Shui-an.

When T'ou-tzu Ta-tung of Shu-chou heard someone quote Zen master Ta-sui's words, "It goes along," he lit some incense, made a deep bow in the direction of Ta-sui's temple, and said, "An old buddha has appeared in Western Shu."[29]

See how a clear-sighted Zen master is able to perceive everything at a single glance without the slightest error? Just like the famous mirror of the Chin Emperor which reflected all one's vital organs.

Once when Tung-shan Hsiao-ts'ung had just started training under Zen master Wen-chu Ying-hsin, Wen-chu posed the following question to instruct his monks: "Straight hooks catch black dragons. Bent hooks catch frogs and earthworms. Has anyone hooked a dragon?" There was a longish pause, then Wen-chu said, "This is a waste of time. The tortoise hair grows longer by the minute." At those words, Hsiao-ts'ung had a sudden realization.[30]

Later, while Hsiao-ts'ung was at Mount Yün-chü serving as keeper of lamps, he heard a visiting monk say that the Great Sage of Ssu-chou (an incarnation of the Bodhisattva Kannon) had recently made an appearance in Yang-chou.[31] The monk then asked, "What do you think the Great Sage is up to, appearing in Yang-chou like that?" Hsiao-ts'ung replied, "Even a man of superior attainments has a love of wealth, but he knows the proper way to get it."[32]

Later the same monk reported Hsiao-ts'ung's words to Hsiang An-chu of Lotus Peak. "The descendants of Yün-men are still alive and prospering!" exclaimed Hsiang in astonishment. Although it was late at night, he lit an offering of incense and made deep bows in the direction of Mount Yün-chü.

I have read about Hsiang An-chu. He was a Dharma son of Feng-hsien Tao-shen. A Dharma grandson of Yün-men himself. The sharpness of his Zen activity was unexcelled. He tested it on people for over twenty years, but never found anyone who could stand up to his thrusts. Even if all the buddhas in the ten directions appeared from their countless buddha-lands, emitting boundless radiance, exercising inconceivable powers, employing the eight marvelous virtues inherent in their voices and their four kinds of unhindered eloquence, and preached the Dharma so that it fell like rain, this hard-nosed old saddlehorn of a bonze wouldn't have even turned to look. But now he hears a few words that slipped from Hsiao-ts'ung's mouth and immediately he lights incense and prostrates himself in the direction of Hsiao-ts'ung's temple. Why? What can it mean? The words Hsiao-ts'ung uttered are found in the Confucian Analects.[33] Hsiang must have known them. Yet when he heard them he was bowled over in amazement. He went into transports of joy. Had he taken leave of his senses? Could it be that he was just stupid? Or, on the other hand, perhaps there is something here that we should greatly value. Certainly, it is a matter for us to deeply ponder.

Once while Zen master Fo-yen Ch'ing-yüan was serving at the Lung-men-ssu Temple one of the monks was bitten by a snake. The master took the incident up as he was teaching in his chambers.[34] "How could a monk of the Dragon Gate (Lung-men) allow himself to be bitten by a snake?" he asked. None of the comments the monks offered were acceptable to Fo-yen. Then Kao-an Shan-wu said, "He displayed all the marks of the great man that he is." The master immediately nodded his affirmation.[35]

When Kao-an's words came to the notice of Zen master Yüan-wu K'o-ch'in at the Chao-chüeh-ssu Temple, he declared in admiration,

"If there's someone like that at Lung-men-ssu, the paths of the East Mountain aren't desolate yet."[36]

Can anyone tell me what Yüan-wu means by *desolate*? Is he describing a state of barrenness, a condition of adversity? Or is he referring to the absence of noise and activity caused by crowds of people?

I've read that "the Buddha's Dharma consists in doing what is right and proper, not in prosperity."[37] So even if a temple were filled with several hundred blind eggplants and gourds [monks] consuming buckets of white rice set before them like hungry wolves or ravenous silkworms, and they were subjected to rigorous discipline, twelve-hour days of zazen without rest, if none of those monks were truly committed to the Way, Yüan-wu would no doubt consider that temple to be barren, in a state of hardship and adversity. But if there was even half a monk, and he was sitting, doggedly doing zazen with his knees bent crookedly and chin pulled in, it wouldn't matter if he were living in a tiny old room with leaky roofs and sodden floors in some dirty, remote back street. If he were single-mindedly committed to penetrating the truth, I guarantee you Yüan-wu would regard that place as rich and flourishing.

This would suggest that what the ancients regarded as lonely and desolate would be considered thriving prosperity by people today, and what people today regard as thriving prosperity would have been considered lonely and desolate by the ancients. How can our school have fallen into such grievous decline?

5

The True and Untransmittable Dharma

Huang-lung Hui-nan, a Dharma heir of Tz'u-ming
Ch'u-yüan, received his initial certification from Master Le-t'an
Huai-ch'eng.[1] He then set out, full of enthusiasm and supremely self-
confident, at the head of a group of monks going around on pilgrimage to visit other teachers. In the course of his travels, he chanced to
encounter the monk Yün-feng Wen-yüeh, and together they went to
visit Mount Hsi. One night as they were talking, Yün-feng asked
Hui-nan about the teaching he had received from Master Le-t'an.
After Hui-nan had explained the essentials of Le-t'an's Zen, Yün-
feng said, "Le-t'an may belong to the lineage of Master Yün-men, but
the way the two men express the Dharma is completely different."

Asked to explain the difference, Yün-feng continued, "Yün-men
is like a pill of immortality, refined nine times over into perfect trans-
parency: it can transform iron into gold. Le-t'an is like quicksilver,
all right to amuse yourself with, but it dissipates the moment it enters
the furnace."

Hui-nan, bristling at this reference to his teacher, picked up a
wooden pillow and threw it angrily at Yün-feng.

The next morning, Yün-feng apologized to Hui-nan, but he went
on to state, "Yün-men has a greatness of spirit like that of a king. Do
you think such a man would allow dead words to pass from his lips?

I'm sure that Le-t'an has attained realization, but his utterances have no life in them. If the words he speaks are dead, how can he hope to instill life in his students?"

He turned and began to leave, but Hui-nan stopped him and demanded, "Who do you consider a good teacher?"

"Tz'u-ming Ch'u-yüan," he replied. "His methods of dealing with students far surpass all other teachers of today. If you're going to visit him, you shouldn't waste any more time."

Hui-nan silently pondered Yün-feng's words: This is the very reason why I left my teacher and came on this pilgrimage. Yün-feng did his training under master Ts'ui-yen, yet still he's urging me to see Tz'u-ming. He assures me I will benefit from it. What would he have to gain if I did go and study with Tz'u-ming?

He readied his traveling pack that very day and set out for Tz'u-ming's temple on Mount Shih-shuang.

You monks pay close attention to this. The ancients never engaged in deception, neither of themselves nor of others. But today's priests? They cling mulishly to old views and opinions, using the teachings their master transmits to them as a crutch. In order to save face, they go to great lengths to put their own lack of attainment in the best possible light. If they persist like this in deceiving themselves, when will the students who come to study with them ever achieve their goal?

Later, when Hui-nan listened to Tz'u-ming teach and heard him disparage almost every Zen teacher around the country, pointing out their errors and showing where each one of them went wrong, he realized that the matters Tz'u-ming was holding up to censure were the very ones that Le-t'an had privately transmitted to him.

He left Tz'u-ming's temple in fallen spirits, but when he recalled what Yün-feng had told him about Tz'u-ming's teaching ability, he had a change of heart. He asked himself, "Should someone who is determined to resolve the Great Matter of life and death allow doubts to remain in his mind?" and hurried back to Tz'u-ming's chambers.

"I'm ignorant and inexperienced," he told Tz'u-ming. "Although I hope to attain the Way, I haven't made much progress. Hearing your teaching last night, I felt like a man who had obtained a compass to guide him after having lost his way. Please have pity on me. Teach me and help me to dispel the doubts in my mind."

Tz'u-ming laughed. "We know about you in the training halls, Librarian Hui-nan. You've been going around visiting Zen teachers with a group of monks. If you have doubts, why carry them with you until you grow old and allow them to sap your energy? Why don't you stay here with me and train for a while so we can thrash out those doubts of yours?"

Tz'u-ming summoned an attendant and had a chair brought out for Hui-nan to sit on. But Hui-nan refused it, and implored Tz'u-ming even more urgently for his help.

"Being a student of Yün-men's Zen," said Tz'u-ming, "you must be familiar with its basic principles. You remember when Yün-men spared Shou-ch'u three beatings with his staff? Do you think Shou-ch'u should have received those blows? Or do you think it was all right that he didn't receive them?"[2]

"He should have received them, of course," Hui-nan replied. Tz'u-ming's countenance turned grave. "You hear the word *staff*," he said, "and immediately you conclude that he should be receiving blows from it. In that case, Shou-ch'u would have to receive blows from sunup to sundown, every time a crow cawed, a magpie screeched, the temple bell rang, or the wooden block was struck. Yün-men would have to be swatting him nonstop, wouldn't he."

Hui-nan just stared uncomprehendingly, so Tz'u-ming said, "When I first saw you, I wasn't at all sure that I could teach you. Now I know that I can." He let Hui-nan perform the formal bows that made him a disciple. As Hui-nan rose from the bows, Tz'u-ming continued, "If you really understand the meaning of Yün-men's Zen, you should be able to tell me this. When Chao-chou met the old woman at Mount T'ai, he said that he saw right through her. What was it he saw through?"[3]

Hui-nan's face reddened. He broke into a profuse sweat. He didn't have the slightest clue how to respond. Deeply humiliated, he jumped up and bolted from the room.

The following day, when Hui-nan went to Tz'u-ming, he was greeted with a fresh round of abuse. Sheepishly avoiding Tz'u-ming's gaze, Hui-nan said, "It's precisely because I don't know that I've come here to find an answer. Do you call it compassion, to treat students like this? How can the Dharma be conferred in such a manner?"

Tz'u-ming just laughed. As he did, Hui-nan suddenly grasped his meaning. "You were right!" he shouted, "Those are dead words Le-t'an speaks!" He composed a verse and presented it to Tz'u-ming,

> Chao-chou stood at the pinnacle of the Zen world,
> No wonder he saw the old woman's true colors,
> Today the whole world has a mirrorlike clarity;
> Pilgrims, don't regard the Way as your enemy.

Hui-nan was thirty-five years old. Do you see how bitter the hardships were the ancients endured when they committed themselves to the study of Zen? Hui-nan emerged like a magnificent phoenix from a stinking owl's egg and soared up into the sky. The two lines of Lin-chi Zen that he and Yang-ch'i Fang-hui established branched out from master Tz'u-ming like the forked tail on a swallow.

At the start of Hsin-ching K'o-wen's career, when he went to Hsiang-ch'eng to visit Priest Shang-lan, Shang-lan asked him where he had come from. "I came from Hui-nan," he replied. "What's Hui-nan telling his monks these days?" asked Shang-lan.

Do you see that? If it had been a training hall in one of today's temples, the question would have been, "How many sticks of incense does Hui-nan sit through these days?" "How many sutras does he recite?" "What Buddhist image does he venerate?" "What precepts does he observe?" What was Shang-lan up to, do you suppose, asking right off, "What's Hui-nan telling his monks these days?"

Hsin-ching said, "Recently, Priest Hui-nan received a request from the prefectural authorities asking him to select someone from his assembly for the abbotship of the Huang-po-ssu Temple. He composed a verse,

> Reciting sutras up in the bell tower;
> Planting greens below the zazen seat.

Then he told his monks, "Anyone who can come up with a comment that matches the meaning in that verse will leave here today to be abbot at Huang-po-ssu."

In another case long ago, an ascetic monk named Ssu-ma traveled all the way from Hunan to visit the great teacher Po-chang.[4] When he met the master, he said, "The scenery at Mount Kuei [Kuei-shan] is exceptionally fine. I bet you could get fifteen hundred monks to train there."

Po-chang said, "If any monk in my assembly can produce a genuine turning verse, I'll send him to Mount Kuei to be head priest." Pointing to a water jar, he said, "You can't call that a water jar. What do you call it?"

His head monk at the time, named Hua-lin, came forward and said, "It can't be called a gate latch." But Po-chang would not accept that answer.

Po-chang posed the question to Ling-yu [later called Zen master Kuei-shan], who was serving as the temple cook. Ling-yu went to the water jar and kicked it over.

"The head monk has lost out to the cook," said Po-chang with a laugh. Thus Ling-yu was made abbot of the temple on Mount Kuei.

Today, when Zen people go about choosing a head priest, they ask him where he comes from. They want to know about his family and career. They want to know how much financial help he can provide. How much money his relatives have. Can he compose good verse? Does he have a good prose style? This candidate has the right looks, but he's too short. That one is tall enough, but he doesn't have the right looks. This fellow's a good calligrapher, but that one's a better speaker. And so they deliberate on and on, leading themselves into ever-deepening ignorance. How welcome it is, then, to find a person who doesn't go slinging feculence around like that, but simply asks his monks for a verse.

[Hsin-ching continued his story to Shang-lan's assembly:] Head monk Wei-sheng offered a comment on Hui-nan's verse: "A ferocious tiger sits blocking the way." Hui-nan accepted it and Wei-sheng became the head priest at Huang-po-ssu.

A monk in the assembly, named Shun, hearing this story, suddenly blurted out, "Head monk Wei-sheng may have received the abbotship for that phrase, but he didn't know the first thing about the Buddha's Dharma!"

Upon hearing those words, Hsin-ching attained great enlightenment and saw with perfect clarity the Zen activity at work in Hui-nan's verse.

When Zen students in former times committed themselves to penetrating the depths, they didn't choose a temple because it was popular with other monks; they didn't care if the training hall was full or not. Their minds were fixed on only one thing: resolving the Great Matter.

Zen people today, being unable to tell slave from master, common stones from jades, can only prattle. They say things like: "Priest So-and-so treats his monks as solicitously as nurslings." "Priest B regards prostrations before Buddhist images as the very heart of Buddhist practice." "Priest C takes only one meal each day." "Priest D sits long periods at a stretch without ever lying down—he's a living buddha."

What has the Zen school come to!

Long ago during the Southern Sung dynasty, Zen master Mi-an Hsien-chieh, a native of the state of Min, was crossing the mountains into Wu-chou to visit the teacher Chih-che Yüan-an. One day, as he was sitting warming himself in the sun, he was approached by an elderly monk who was obviously a veteran of the Dharma wars. "Where will you go when you leave here?" the monk asked him.

"I'm going to Ssu-mei to visit Fo-chih T'uan-yü at the monastery at Mount A-yü-wang," Mi-an replied. "When the country falls into spiritual decline, even young monks on pilgrimage are affected," said the monk. "They pay attention to what they hear, but neglect what they see."

"What do you mean?" demanded Mi-an. The monk replied, "There are currently a thousand monks residing at Mount A-yü-wang. The abbot can't possibly give personal instruction to each one. Do you think he's going to find time to work with someone like you, who's making out all right on his own?"

"Then where am I to go?" said Mi-an, tears appearing in his eyes. "There's a priest named Ying-an T'an-hua in Mei-kuo, Ch'u-chou. He's young, but his discernment is second to none. Go see him."

Mi-an followed the monk's advice. He studied under Ying-an for four years, in the course of which he was able to break through and grasp the vital life-source of the buddha-patriarchs.

Practicers today move around from temple to temple looking for a place that offers them comfortable living conditions and serves them bowls of thick gruel at mealtimes. They don't give much thought to the problem of birth and death, or to penetrating the secret depths. They come wandering into temples like herds of deer; they come filing in like a swarm of ants. There is a world of difference between practitioners like them and a true seeker like Mi-an.

Priest Wu-tsu Fa-yen once addressed the following remarks to his pupils:

> Back twenty or thirty years ago, I traveled around the country looking for a teacher. After I had spent some time practicing under several experienced masters, I thought my study was over. But when I reached Mount Fu and joined the assembly under master Yüan-chien, I found that I couldn't even open my mouth. After that, while I was practicing under Master Po-yün, I got my teeth into an iron bun. When I was finally able to chew it, I discovered it possessed hundreds of marvelous flavors. How would I express that? I'd say,
>
> > The flowers on the cockscomb crown the early autumn;
> > Who dyed the purple in their splendid silken heads?
> > Soon winds will come, their combs will brush together,
> > An endless struggle will unfold before the temple stairs.

Did you hear him? "I thought my training was over." Now if Fa-yen, when he believed his practice was at an end, had not entered Yüan-chien's chambers, and had not come under Po-yün's wing, he might have carried his mistakes around with him to the grave. What a precious thing a Zen teacher is whose eyes are truly open. A priceless treasure not only for men, but for devas as well. But even that remains unknown to those today who throw their lives away by supposing prematurely they have concluded their training.

One day early in Fa-yen's career, when he was studying under Yüan-chien, Yüan-chien told him, "I'm not getting any younger. By staying here with me, you may be wasting valuable time. I want you to go to Po-yün Shou-tuan. He's young in years, and I've never actually met him, but judging from the verse comment he made on the three blows Lin-chi received from Huang-po, he's an exceptional monk.[5] If you study with him, I'm sure you'll be able to bring your Great Matter to completion."

Fa-yen knew in his heart the truth of his teacher's words. He bade him farewell and set out for Mount Po-yün.

What magnanimity! Yüan-chien's total selflessness deserves our deepest respect. How different from the Zen teachers today! When they certify a student, they hand him a piece of paper containing a line of two of some lifeless words they have written on it, telling him, "You are like this. I am like this too. Preserve it carefully. Never change or deviate from it."

Students receive these certificates with deep bows of gratitude, raise them over their heads in attitudes of reverence. They guard them religiously all their sleeping and waking hours until the day they die—and in the process they make a total waste of their lives. Their own true face remains forever unknown to them. The reason why Yüan-chien chose Po-yün's temple to send Fa-yen to is because he was suspicious of prosperous training halls that were filled with monks, and because his sole concern was to keep the true Zen wind from dying out.

One day, when Fa-yen was working as head of the milling shed, one of the monks suddenly pointed to the turning millstone and said, "Does that move by supernatural power? Or does it move naturally?" Fa-yen hitched up his robe and made a circumambulation of the stone. The monk said nothing.

Later, Master Po-yün came into the shed and spoke to Fa-yen. "I had some monks here visiting from Mount Lu. They had all experienced enlightenment. When I asked them to express their understanding, they did it very well, with words of substance. When I questioned them about episodes involving Zen masters of the past, they were able to clarify them. When I requested comments on Zen sayings, the comments they supplied were perfectly acceptable. In spite of all that, they still weren't there yet."[6]

Po-yün's words brought deep doubts to Fa-yen's mind. "They had achieved enlightenment," he pondered. "They were able to express their understanding. They could clarify the stories the master gave them. Why did he say they still lacked something?" After struggling with this for several days, he suddenly broke through into enlightenment. Everything that had seemed so precious to him was now cast aside, as he raced to Po-yün's chambers. When Po-yün saw him, he got up and began dancing about for him, waving his arms and stamping his feet. Fa-yen just looked on and laughed.

Afterward, Fa-yen said, "I broke into great beads of sweat . . . then suddenly I experienced for myself 'the fresh breeze that rises up when the great burden is laid down.' "[7]

We must prize Fa-yen's example. After only a few days of intense effort, he transcended in one leap all the gradual stages of attainment—the Three Wisdoms and the Four Fruits—and penetrated directly the hearts of all the twenty-eight Indian and the six Chinese Zen patriarchs. After that, he spoke with effortless freedom whenever he opened his mouth, taking students completely unaware when he responded to their questions, and cutting the ground from under them with his own questions. Reflect deeply, and you will see that this is the very point at which men of great stature surpass the countless ranks of average men; and it is at this same point that the lax and indolent lose hope.

Long ago, Emperor Yü saved a hundred provinces from the ravages of flood by having a passage cut open for the Yellow River at the Dragon Gates. But the project took years, required the forced labor of countless men and women, and cost many of them their lives. Emperor Kao-tsung struggled through a period of great upheaval to establish the foundations for a dynasty of Han rulers that endured for four centuries. But the policies he initiated during the forty years of his reign resulted in death and suffering for untold millions of his subjects. What these two emperors accomplished has made their names known throughout the world. Yet their achievements were defiled by the illusory passions that engendered them. The difference between such worldly achievements and the spiritual exploits of a Zen teacher like Fa-yen, which were utterly free of the defiling passions, is vaster than the difference between sky and sea.

Unfortunately, however, we have another species of teacher in our Zen school. The kind who puffs up self-importantly when he's able to round up seven or eight monks. He stalks like a tiger with a mean glint in his eye. Parades around like an elephant with his nose stuck proudly in the air. He delivers smug judgments:

> Master So-and-so is an excellent priest. His poems are reminiscent of Li Yu-lin. Writes prose like Yüan Chung-lang. And the ample fare you get in his temple cannot be matched anywhere else in the country. There is a morning meal, a midday meal, tea and cakes three times a day. Before the afternoon tea-break is even over, the

board sounds announcing the evening meal. The master teaches the Dharma of "direct pointing" itself, and ushers students into enlightenment with no more effort than it takes to pick up a clod of dirt at the roadside. Mr. Kobayashi's third son went to him and was immediately enlightened. Mr. Suzuki's fourth son went and grasped the Dharma right off. Samurais and farmers, artisans and merchants, even butchers, innkeepers, peddlers, and everyone else who passes through the gates of his temple—he leads them all straight into the realm of truth. I don't know of a training hall in the world to compare with it. Any monk on pilgrimage who fails to enter So-and-so's gate is making the mistake of a lifetime; he is throwing his search for satori right out the window.

Phffmp! What graveyard did you pillage for those old left-over offerings? Who did you get that line about "direct pointing" from? How can you say that enlightenment comes as effortlessly as "picking up a clod of dirt"? Are you really talking about the "secret transmission" of the Sixth Patriarch? The "essential matter" Lin-chi transmitted? If it was as easy as you say it is, and it was enough for a student merely to receive and accept a teaching after his teacher explained it to him, why do Zen people speak of the "wondrous Dharma that the buddhas and patriarchs do not transmit"?

One day long ago when Zen master Hsiang-yen Chih-kuan was studying under Kuei-shan Ling-yu, Ling-yu addressed the following question to him: "I've heard you have a brilliant mind. They say you're so perceptive that when you were with your late teacher Po-chang you gave answers of ten when he asked about one, and answers of a hundred when he asked about ten. But that intellectual sharpness and perceptiveness is the very source of birth and death. What I want from you right now is a single phrase that comes from a time prior to your birth."

Chih-kuan, utterly confused, returned to the monks' quarters in a daze. He took out the writings he had been studying and began to comb them for a phrase he could take back to Ling-yu. But he was unable to come up with a single one. He sighed to himself, "You can't satisfy hunger with a painted rice cake."

He begged Ling-yu for some clue that would help him answer. "If

I told you something now," Ling-yu replied, "later you would curse me to your dying day. Whatever I said would be mine, it would have nothing to do with you."

Chih-kuan ended up taking all his writings and study-notes and tossing them into the fire. "I'll never study Zen again in this lifetime," he said. "I think I'll go on an extended pilgrimage. I can beg my way as a mendicant monk. At least I can avoid wearing myself out like I'm doing now."

He took leave of Ling-yu with tears in his eyes, and made straight for the Hsiang-yen-ssu Temple in Nan-yang to pay homage at the memorial tower of National Master Hui-chung.[8] When he got there, he decided to stay for a while and rest up from his long journey.

One day, Chih-kuan was out clearing away some brush and weeds. His sickle struck a pebble, throwing it against the trunk of a bamboo with a sharp *toc.* At that instant, he attained enlightenment. He hurried back to the monks' quarters and washed to purify himself, then he lit some incense and bowed deeply in the direction of the temple on far-off Mount Kuei where Ling-yu resided. "The gratitude I owe you for your great compassion is far greater than that I owe my own parents," he said. "If you had given in to my pleas that day and said something to help me, this moment would never have arrived."

Do you see? The masters of our school have never imparted one shred of Dharma to their students. Not because they were worried about protecting the Dharma, but because they were worried about protecting their students.

The monks that teachers must deal with today are generally ignorant, stubborn, unmotivated types who aren't even up to sitting through a single stick of incense. They teach these people and nurse them along with tender care. But they might as well take a load of dead cow-heads, line them up, and try to get them to eat grass. The teachers muck about, doing this and trying that, endeavoring to get these fellows free of themselves. Instead, they end up saddling them with an enormous load of shit. Then they sanction them, give them fine certificates of enlightenment, and loose them upon the world. The difference between such teachers and priests like Ling-yu and Chih-kuan is a difference of mud and cloud.

If anyone tells you, "I can preach a Dharma that will enlighten people," you can be sure of two things: one, he is not an authentic teacher, and two, he himself has never penetrated the Dharma. Even if he possessed the wisdom of Shariputra and the eloquence of Purna, he couldn't possibly get his miserable beak into the wondrous untransmittable essence that Zen teachers have transmitted through the centuries from Dharma father to Dharma son.

The venerable Ananda was a cousin of the Buddha. He followed him into the priesthood at a young age and became his personal attendant, in which capacity he served constantly at the Buddha's side. So not only was he habitually exposed to the Tathagata's virtuous influence for many years, he was also no doubt affected in no small measure by the personal instruction he must have received. In spite of that, Ananda was never able to break through the barrier into enlightenment. It was not until after the Buddha's death, when he went to his fellow disciple Kashyapa to continue his study, that he succeeded in "forgetting his self and yielding up his life."

In light of all this, how is it that enlightenment, which was so difficult for the ancients to achieve, is now so effortlessly attained by the moderns? Could it be that the ancients were weak or lacked ability? Could it be that today's students are more mature and highly developed? Could it be that the teaching methods the ancients used were inferior to those of today?

Hui-k'o cut off one of his arms. Tz'u-ming jabbed a gimlet into his thigh. Another monk did zazen constantly without ever lying down to rest. Another shut himself up in a hermitage and never left it. Why did they subject themselves to such adversity? If the easy enlightenment of the moderns is genuine, the hardships the ancients endured was mistaken. If the hardships the ancients endured was not mistaken, there is something wrong with the enlightenment of the moderns.

It is unavoidable if a person of great resolve strives to break through to enlightenment and fails. But once someone vows to achieve enlightenment, no matter what hardships he may face, even if it takes him thirty or even forty years of arduous effort, he should without fail achieve his goal and reach the ground of awakening that was realized and confirmed by Zen patriarchs before him. How can that same ground be reached by any of these moderns who live in a half-drunk, half-sober state, misusing their lives because they trust to a common, ignorant view that believes enlightenment is attained effortlessly, like picking up clods of dirt from the ground? Are such people any different from the man of Ch'i, who ran to the cemetery when he was hungry to beg leftovers from the worshipers?[9]

It is because of this that Seng-chao states in *The Treatise of the Precious Treasury*:

> There are ten thousand ways leading to enlightenment. A fish that grows weary remains in a trickling stream. A sick bird alights and stays among the reeds. The one never knows the immensity of the ocean, the other never knows the vastness of the great forests. It is the same for practicers who turn aside from the great Way and enter small, insignificant bypaths. After striving and acquiring a certain amount of merit, they stop while they are still halfway to their destination and thus never reach the final truth of ultimate suchness. By forsaking the great Way in order to pursue small, insignificant bypaths, and contenting themselves with a small measure of attainment, they never reach the complete satisfaction of great and ultimate peace.

Who are the people who pursue the "great Way"? Those true seekers who achieve an authentic *kenshō* and bore all the way through into the profound source of the great Dharma. Who are those who pursue the "small and insignificant bypaths"? Pseudo-Zennists who accept their perceptions and sensory awareness, their seeing and hearing, as some kind of ultimate attainment.

Seng-chao was indeed a man of superior capacity, one of those he himself called "authentic vessels of the Mahayana Dharma." He lived during the latter Chin dynasty, before the First Patriarch came from the West and brought Zen to China. He stood alone amid a vast ocean of uncertain Buddhist doctrine and expounded a profound, perfectly correct Dharma of unsurpassable greatness. There is a world of difference between him and Zen people today. It is like comparing gold with tin, or masters with servants. He deserves our profoundest respect.

Ch'ing-su, a monk from Ku-t'ien in the kingdom of Min, served as an attendant to Tz'u-míng.[10] In his later years he took refuge in Lu-yüan, Hsiang-hsi, living by himself and leading a quiet, retired existence. Tou-shuai Ts'ung-yüeh, who was still a student at the time, was occupying a neighboring dwelling. One day, a visitor brought Tou-shuai some litchis. He called to Ch'ing-su, "Someone brought me some fruit from your home province, old man. Let's share them."

"I haven't seen any litchis since my teacher passed away," Ch'ing-su replied with an air of sadness. "Who was your teacher?" asked Tou-shuai. "Master Tz'u-ming," he replied.

When he had a chance, Tou-shuai invited Ch'ing-su over and questioned him further about his life and practice. Ch'ing-su in turn asked Tou-shuai whom he had studied with. "Hsin-ching K'o-wen," he said. "Who was his teacher?" asked Ch'ing-su. "Huang-lung Hui-nan," answered Tou-shuai.

"Young Hui-nan was only with Tz'u-ming a short time," said Ch'ing-su, "yet he and his disciples now are enjoying great success."

The remark surprised Tou-shuai. "This is no ordinary old monk," he thought to himself. Later, putting some incense into his sleeve, he went to Ch'ing-su and asked for his instruction.

"A man of my meager virtues, who doesn't get a chance to meet people, really shouldn't presume to teach others," said Ch'ing-su. "But if that's what you want, why don't you express the understanding you have attained as straightforwardly as you can?"

When Tou-shuai finished, Ch'ing-su said, "That may have gained you entrance into the realm of buddhas, but it'll never get you past the gates of Mara's realm. An old worthy said, 'The difficult Barrier is not reached until you utter an Ultimate Word'[11]—that is something you still have to learn."

Tou-shuai was about to reply to this, but Ch'ing-su suddenly asked, "How would you say something without working your mouth?" Once again Tou-shuai started to speak, but Ch'ing-su cut him off with a high-pitched laugh. Tou-shuai was suddenly enlightened.

Several months later, Ch'ing-su certified Tou-shuai's enlightenment. He added a caution: "Everything Hsin-ching taught you was perfectly true and correct, but you left him much too soon, before you had finally grasped the marvelous working in his Zen teaching. What I've done now is to reveal that working to you and enable you to use it freely and unrestrictedly. But I don't want you to stay here and become my Dharma heir. Your teacher is Hsin-ching." Eventually, Tou-shuai did receive Hsin-ching's Dharma transmission.

Later, when Layman Wu-chin was studying with Tou-shuai, Tou-shuai mentioned what Ch'ing-su had told him concerning the Ultimate Word. Some time afterward, when Wu-chin resigned from his post as prime minister and was passing the Kui-tsung-ssu Temple where Hsin-ching was living, he stopped to pay him a visit. One night the two men were talking and Wu-chin was telling Hsin-ching what Ch'ing-su had said, when Hsin-ching suddenly flew into a rage. "What a disgusting mess of bloody vomit that bonze spewed out! Don't believe a word of it! It's a pack of lies!" Wu-chin was unable to finish what he was saying.

In the third year of Emperor Hui-tsung's reign (after Hsin-ching had passed away), Chüeh-fan Hui-hung paid a visit to Layman Wu-chin at Ching-hsi in Hsia-chou. Wu-chin said, "It's too bad Hsin-ching didn't perceive Ch'ing-su's true meaning."

"You have only grasped what Ch'ing-su said about the Ultimate Word," said Chüeh-fan. "You have yet to realize that Hsin-ching was dispensing his drastic Zen medicine right before your eyes." "Could that be true?" declared Wu-chin, taken aback. "If you aren't sure, think back. Reflect thoroughly on the meeting you had with Hsin-ching," said Chüeh-fan.

The instant Layman Wu-chin heard Chüeh-fan's words, he discerned the true meaning of Master Hsin-ching's behavior. He lit an offering of incense and prostrated himself in the direction of Kui-tsung-ssu, repenting his mistake and begging the now-deceased Zen teacher for forgiveness. He brought out a portrait of Hsin-ching he had been storing away carefully, made obeisance before it, and inscribed a eulogy above the painting. He presented it to Chüeh-fan.

Ah! Tou-shuai, you had the wisdom to visit Ch'ing-su, and you received his teaching, but you were unable to rid yourself of its traces—all the ruts and grooves it had impressed in your mind. That is the reason why, when Layman Wu-chin came along, he fell right into them. Unless Chüeh-fan had been able to make a good and timely application of Hsin-ching's drastic medicine, Wu-chin would never have recovered from the incurable illness he had contracted.[12]

Each Zen master possesses ways and methods all his own of applying his wisdom to benefit his students and bring them to realization. How can others possibly hope to calculate their limitless scope?

My own opinion is this: while the above assessment may well be true, I still think it is regrettable that when Chüeh-fan revealed to Wu-chin the drastic medicine Hsin-ching had used, it seems to have worked with no more strength than a punctured drum.

A superior man of Layman Wu-chin's caliber is rarely seen in the world. He rose to become chief minister of state, and lived to be nearly a hundred years old. He won the emperor's complete trust, was highly esteemed by the ministers under him, deeply respected by the educated classes, and beloved by the common people. His wisdom was unsurpassed, his benevolence was vast, a man worthy to serve at the emperor's side. Zen master Chüeh-fan made a special trip just to see him. Zen master Ta-hui also traveled far in order to pay him a visit. What mistake could a man of his stature have committed that would bring him, when he recalled Hsin-ching's angry outburst, to go into the starry night, light incense, and bow penitently in the direction of Kui-tsung-ssu? Everyone who belongs to the school of Zen should understand: there exists in our school an essential matter that can only be penetrated in great enlightenment.

When Po-chang's nose was tweaked by Ma-tsu, it cost him all the peace and equanimity he had previously attained. When Lin-chi was struck by Huang-po's fist, he lost both home and country. When Feng-hsüeh's pride was crushed by Nan-yüan, it stripped his face right off. When Hsüeh-feng heard Yen-t'ou's "Khat!" it drained his spirit dry. When Yün-men got shoved out the door and broke his leg, it stunned him senseless. For Chih-kuan, it was a pebble striking a bamboo. For Tz'u-ming, it was Fen-yang's hand over his mouth, muffling him. Ts'ui-yen was done in by a piece of broken tile. Yüan-wu was moved to tears by a love poem. Ta-yüan's heart was destroyed by the sounds from a flute. Ta-hui was struck down by the poisonous heat of a south wind.[13]

The circumstances through which these priests came into their own, by forgetting what happened in the Himalayas when the World-honored One was caught in the light of a poisonous star,[14] is something even the devas and devil kings cannot discern.

When Su-shan heard Chih-kuan state that "words are produced by means of sounds, but sounds are not words; forms and shapes appear to be real, but they are not," he thought that Chih-kuan had thoroughly articulated the Dharma truth. So when it came time for him to leave Chih-kuan, he made him a promise: "I'll wait until you have become abbot, then I'll return to the temple to gather fuel and draw water for you."

But later, when Su-shan came up against Ming-chao Te-chien, he suffered a severe setback. He realized for the first time how circumstances really are among followers of Zen. Upon returning to Chih-kuan and hearing him teach his students, he was overcome with disgust—the way a highly cultured minister might feel listening to the uncouth banter of a peasant. He made gagging noises as though he were vomiting. He had given his word to serve as Chih-kuan's disciple because he had believed him to be the only genuinely enlightened member of Ling-yu's brotherhood. Now, since he was able to see the true content of Chih-kuan's teaching, everything had changed completely.

I want all of you to be aware that the study of Zen can effect a miraculous transformation that will change you to the very marrow of your bones. If Su-shan had not clambered his way arduously up the complicated tangle of vines Ming-chao had lowered down for him, how could he ever have matured into the great vessel he later became?

When Lung-ya was struck by Zen master Lin-chi, he said, "If you want to hit me, go ahead, but I still say there's no meaning in the First Patriarch's coming from the West." When he was hit by Zen master Ts'ui-wei, again he said, "If you want to hit me, go ahead, but I still say there's no meaning in the First Patriarch's coming from the West." Where Lung-ya stood, he saw no buddhas above him, no sentient beings below him; there was no sky over his head or earth beneath his feet. The whole universe, the great earth—it was all a single holeless iron hammer. Hence Hsüeh-tou dubbed him "a blind dragon for whom neither seer nor seen exists."[15] The regrettable truth of the matter is, Lung-ya could not have grasped Lin-chi's Zen even in his dreams.

Lung-ya had come down with a grave illness, one that the buddhas and patriarchs themselves cannot cure. Often students latch onto a pile of matted filth like Lung-ya did and joyously assume they have obtained the very heart of the ancestral teachers, the "priceless jewel" *The Lotus Sutra* says is "concealed in the lining of your robe." Their misfortune is, they haven't the faintest notion that what they have really obtained are the same filthy nails and wedges that Master Yün-men was constantly working to *pull out* for his students.

Even if they realize that the nails and wedges are there, and attempt to remove them on their own, they only end up like Papiyas, the devil king, who proudly went around sporting a stinking dog's corpse on his head. When the corpse was first placed there by Upagupta, the Fourth Indian Patriarch, Papiyas danced with delight, thinking to himself, "What a glorious adornment I have! Now there's no reason for me to envy the headdresses of Brahma or Indra." But when he returned to his palace, his wives fled, pinching their noses, avoiding him with their faces contorted in disgust. Only then did he realize that his headdress consisted of three maggot-ridden corpses—a man, a dog, and a snake. The devil king was bewildered and demoralized, and tormented by the anger and resentment that burned within him.

Much the same thing happens to a Zen student. He encounters a Zen master and sees his assertions demolished. He receives the master's instruction and, eventually, he receives his confirmation. When that happens, he assumes, "I have attained my goal, concluded the Great Matter. The buddha-patriarchs themselves have nothing for me to envy."

Unfortunately, in the end his views become distorted, withering into dry, stale things. He discovers that he is at odds with himself at all times, whether active or at rest. The light that seems to have come into his darkness shines without a trace of strength, so he lives down in a jackal den, or dwells in a cavern of disembodied spirits, burdened by an iron yoke around his neck and heavy shackles around his arms and legs.

Someone with a true Dharma eye sees this as a scene of total and unrelieved despair. Because the student will never understand Zen, not in his dreams, not if he waits until the Year of the Ass.[16] On the contrary, before he knows it he is lying among the other burnt-out seeds, rotting away, incapable of generating new life. Isn't he a man walking around with a dog's carcass on his head? He could run off to the ends of the earth looking for a way to rid himself of his burden, but meantime the rot would only worsen, the stench would only grow more loathsome. When will he ever be free of it? What can he possibly do?

Well, if a person really has a mind to reach the basic ground that has been realized and confirmed by the Zen patriarchs, it is by no means impossible. As a start, he should work on the koan Does a Dog Have the Buddha-nature? If he concentrates on it single-mindedly and keeps at it for a long time without wavering or faltering, he is certain to break through to realization. He must not stop there, however. He must cast all that he has attained aside, and turn to tackle one of the difficult-to-pass koans. If he proceeds in this way, he will surely come to see that the ground where the ancients lived and functioned is not found at any level of intellectual understanding.

Hsi-keng was initially enlightened when he penetrated the koan of The Old Sail Not Yet Raised. But he didn't rest content with that first realization, he went on and introspected Su-shan's Memorial Tower for four more years. Only when he had penetrated that koan did he develop into a great Dharma vessel. Had he stopped at that point, and dwelled where, as he said, "there is nowhere on earth to put it," he would have remained floating aimlessly on a vast expanse of stagnant water, a dead lump of rotting flesh even a decrepit old crow wouldn't have given a second look. If that had happened, do you think he would have developed into a great Zen master? Someone who was sought out to serve as abbot at ten different Zen temples and monasteries?[17]

Here is where the secret to the final breakthrough is found. A great deal has been said about it, most of it mistaken, much of it irresponsible nonsense. Daitō Kokushi said, "In the morning our eyebrows meet; in the evening we brush shoulders. What do I look like?"[18] Those words are extremely difficult to place your trust in, extremely difficult to grasp. Kanzan Kokushi said, "Chao-chou's koan The Cypress Tree in the Garden contains a vital function that works like a bandit."[19] Those words are likewise exceedingly difficult to penetrate and pass into. We must revere the deep compassion of these two Zen teachers, who left behind these hidden keys to total transformation so they would be there when a descendant appeared with the capacity to grasp them. Their utterances are truly the claws and fangs of the Dharma cave.

Once a person has bored his way into them, once his body has been covered with white beads of sweat, then he may rightly call himself a descendant of Hsi-keng, one of those Hsi-keng said "would be appearing daily in the land beyond the Eastern Sea."[20] If, on the other hand, he finds that he hesitates or vacillates, and is unable to pass through them, he must never claim that he is a descendant of Kanzan Kokushi.

Today, wherever you go, Zen priests say, "Words and letters. Zen phrases. Those are the tools of slaves and servants. I don't have any use for them."

Wrong! Dead wrong! Are those two great Zen masters slaves or servants? If they are, I'm one too. While I don't care much for the high and mighty attitude that makes those priests look down on others as their inferiors, I don't despise them for it either. However, they are supposed to be descendants of Daitō and Kanzan, and as such, they should be able to penetrate their utterances. Otherwise, what right have they to refer to themselves as "small fish inhabiting the ocean of the true Dharma"?

If a person has not penetrated these sayings, then even if he has achieved attainment, even if his practice is single-minded, he should still, without further thought, just take them and begin to introspect them; he should abandon himself to the task with total concentration and relentless effort.

It's like chopping down a huge tree of immense girth. You won't accomplish it with one swing of your axe. If you keep chopping away at it, though, and do not let up, eventually, whether it wants to or not, it will suddenly topple down. When that time comes, you could round up everyone you could find and pay them to hold the tree up, but they wouldn't be able to do it. It would still come crashing to the ground.

A person may not be ruined because he commits a single wrong act, but if he persists in doing wrong, it will eventually bring about his downfall, whether he wants it or not. When that time comes, he will not be able to prevent it even if he goes to all the gods of heaven and earth and begs with tears in his eyes for their help.

Introspecting a koan is like that. It isn't a question of choosing a koan, scrutinizing it once, and penetrating it. If you work on it relentlessly, with unflagging devotion, you will penetrate it whether you want to or not. When that time comes, even the combined effort of all the devil kings in the ten directions could not prevent it from happening. Why they couldn't even glimpse what was going on. And there is nothing that could bring you such intense joy and satisfaction!

But if the woodcutter stopped after one or two strokes of his axe to ask the third son of Mr. Chang, "Why doesn't this tree fall?" And after three or four more strokes stopped again to ask the fourth son of Mr. Li, "Why doesn't this tree fall?" he would never succeed in felling the tree. It is no different for someone who is practicing the Way.

I haven't been telling you all this in hopes of impressing you with the originality of my ideas. All of the matters I have related here are ones that greatly concerned my teacher Shōju. He was constantly grieving and lamenting over them when I studied with him thirty years ago. I can never tell people about them without finding tears streaming down my old cheeks and dampening my robe. Now, as I recall the earnestness with which old Shōju entrusted his teaching to me, the way he told me how much he was counting on me, I feel an immediate need to run off somewhere and hide my worthlessness. I am divulging my true thoughts to you like this only because I fervently desire that you will expend every effort to make the true, penetrating wind blow once again through the ancestral gardens, and breathe vigorous and enduring strength into the fundamental principles of our school.

Finally, I ask that you overlook once more an old man's foolish grumblings, and thank you all for listening so patiently and attentively during these long talks. Please take good care of yourselves.

The fifth year of Gembun (1740), during the final third of the first month.

Names of Zen Masters and Monks

Bassui Tokushō, 1327–1387
Bodhidharma, d. 532

Chan-t'ang Wen-chun (Tandō Bunjun) 1061–1115
Ch'ang-ch'ing Ta-an (Chōkei Daian) 793–883
Ch'ang-sha Ching-ts'en (Chōsha Keijin) n.d.
Ch'ang-tsung Chao-chüeh (Jōsō Shōgaku) 1025–1091
Chao-chou Ts'ung-shen (Jōshū Jūshin) 778–897
Chao-chüeh: see Ch'ang-tsung Chao-chüeh
Ch'en Tsun-su (Chin Sonshuku) 780–877
Chieh of Mount Wu: see Wu-tsu Shih-chieh
Ch'ien-feng (Kempō) n.d.
Chih-che Yüan-an (Chisha Gen'an) n.d.
Chih-i, T'ien-t'ai master (Chigi) 515–577
Chih-kuan: see Hsiang-yen Chih-kuan
Ch'ing-su, monk (Shōso) n.d.
Ch'ing-yüan Hsing-ssu (Seigan Gyōshi) 660–740
Chiu-feng Tao-ch'ien (Kyūhō Dōken) n.d.
Chu-hung, of Yün-ch'i: see Yün-ch'i Chu-hung
Chüeh-fan Hui-hung (Kakuhan Ekō) 1071–1128
Ch'ung-hsien: see Hsüeh-tou Ch'ung-hsien

Daiō Kokushi: Nampo Jōmyō (1235–1309)
Daitō Kokushi: Shūhō Myōchō (1282–1338)

Engū, n.d.
Enjo, n.d.
Eshin Sōzu (Genshin) 942–1017

Fa-yen: see Wu-tsu Fa-yen
Fen-yang Shan-chao (Fun'yō Zenshō) 947–1024
Feng-hsien Tao-shen (Busen Dōshin) n.d.
Feng-hsüeh Yen-chao (Fūketsu Enshō) 896–973
Fo-chih T'uan-yü (Butchi Tan'yū) 1085–1150

Fo-kuo: see Yüan-wu K'o-ch'in
Fo-yen Ch'ing-yüan (Butsugen Seion) 1067–1120
Fu, senior monk (Fu Jōza) n.d.
Fu-shan Yüan-chien (Fusan Enkan) 991–1067
Fu-yen Liang-ya (Fukugon Ryōga) n.d.

Gokei Sōton (1416–1500)
Gudō Kokushi: Gudō Tōshoku (1579–1661)

Hakuin Ekaku (1685–1768)
Hsi-keng (Sokkō): see Hsü-t'ang Chih-yü
Hsia-tao Hui-yüan (Katsudō Eon) 1103–1176
Hsiao-ying Chung-wen (Gyōei Chūon) 12th c.
Hsiang An-chu (Shō Anju) n.d.
Hsiang-yen Chih-kuan (Kyōgen Chikan) d. 898
Hsiao-ts'ung: see Tung-shan Hsiao-ts'ung
Hsin-ching K'o-wen (Shinjō Kokubun: Kokumon) 1025–1102
Hsin-ju Che: see Ta-kuei Mu-che
Hsü-t'ang Chih-yü (Kidō Chigu) 1185–1269
Hsüeh-feng I-ts'un (Seppō Gizon) 822–908
Hsüeh-tou Ch'ung-hsien (Setchō Juken) 980–1052
Hsui, senior monk (Shū) n.d.
Hua-lin Shan-chüeh (Karin Zenkaku) n.d.
Hua-lin, head monk: see Hua-lin Shan-chüeh
Huang-lung Hui-nan (Ōryō E'nan) 1002–1069
Huang-po Hsi-yun (Ōbaku Kiun) d. mid 9th c.
Hui-ch'iu Shao-lung (Kukyū Jōryū) 1077–1136
Hui-chung: see Nan-yang Hui-chung
Hui-k'o, Second Patriarch (Eka) n.d.
Hui-nan: see Huang-lung Hui-nan
Hui-nan, Librarian: see Huang-lung Hui-nan
Hui-neng, Sixth Patriarch (Enō) 638–713
Hui-t'ang Tsu-hsin (Maidō Sōshin) 1025–1100
Hung-jen, Fifth Patriarch (Gunin) 601–674
Huo-an Shih-t'i (Wakuan Shitai) 1108–1179

I of Tuan-ya: see Tuan-ya Liao-i
Ikkyū Sōjun, 1394–1481

Ju-hui: see Tung-ssu Ju-hui

Kanzan Egen, 1277–1360
Kanzan Kokushi: see Kanzan Egen
Kao-an Shan-wu (Kōan Zengo) 1074–1132
Kao-feng Yüan-miao (Kōhō Gemmyō) 1238–1295
Keisen Sōryū, 1425–1500

Kuei-shan Ling-yu (Isan Reiyū) 771–853

Le-p'u Yüan-an (Rakufu Gen'an) 834–98
Le-t'an Huai-ch'eng (Rokutan Kaichō) n.d.
Lin-chi I-hsüan (Rinzai Gigen) d. 866
Ling-yu: see Kuei-shan Ling-yu
Lo-shan Tao-hsien (Rasan Dōkan) n.d.
Lung-ya Chu-tun (Ryūge Koton) 835–923

Ma-tsu Tao-i (Baso Dōitsu) 709–788
Meng-an Yüan-ts'ung (Mōan Gensō) d. 1209
Mi-an Hsien-chieh (Mittan Kanketsu) 1118–1186
Ming-an, Zen master (Myōan) n.d.
Ming-chao Te-chien (Myōshō Tokken) n.d.
Mu-chou: see Ch'en Tsun-su

Nampo Jōmyō: see Daiō Kokushi
Nan-ch'üan P'u-yüan (Nansen Fugan) 748–835
Nan-hai Tsung-pao (Nankai Sōhō) 13th c.
Nan-t'ung Yüan-ching (Nandō Genjō) 1065–1135
Nan-yang Hui-chung (Nan'yō Echū) d. 775
Nan-yüan Hui-yung (Nan'in Egyō) d. 930
Nan-yüeh Huai-jang (Nangaku Ejō) 677–744

Pa-ling Hao-chien (Haryō Kōkan) n.d.
Pao, senior monk (Hō) n.d.
P'ing, Attendant (Hei) n.d.
P'o-an Tsu-hsien (Hōan Sōsen) 1136–1211
Po-chang Huai-hai (Hyakujō Ekai) 720–814
Po-yün Shou-tuan (Hakuun Shutan) 1025–1072

San-sheng Hui-jan (Sanshō E'nen) n.d.
Sekkō Sōshin, 1408–1486
Seng-chao (Sōjō) 374–414
Seng-ch'ieh (Sanga) 628–710
Shan, Attendant (Zen) n.d.
Shang-lan, priest (Jōran) n.d.
Shidō Mun'an, 1603–1676
Shih-shuang Ch'ing-chu (Sekisō Keisho) 807–888
Shih-t'ou Hsi-ch'ien (Sekitō Kisen) 700–790
Shōju Etan, 1642–1721
Shōju Rōjin: see Shōju Etan
Shou-ch'u: see Tung-shan Shou-ch'u
Shou-shan Sheng-nien (Shuzan Shōnen) 926–993
Shu-chung Wu-yün (Jōchū Muon) 1309–1386
Shūhō Myōchō: see Daitō Kokushi

Shui-an Shih-i (Suian Shiichi) 1107–1176
Shun, monk (Jun) n.d.
Sixth Patriarch: see Hui-neng
Sokkō: see Hsi-keng
Ssu-ma, ascetic monk (Shiba) n.d.
Su-shan Kuang-jen (Sozan Kōnin) 837–909
Sung-yüan Ch'ung-yüeh (Shōgen Sūgaku) 1139–1209

Ta-hui Tsung-kao (Daie Sōkō) 1089–1163
Takuan Sōhō, 1573–1645
Ta-kuei Mu-che (Taii Botetsu) n.d.
Ta-p'ing Hui-ch'in (Taihei Egon) 1059–1117
Ta-sui Fa-chen (Daizui Hōshin) 878–963
Ta-yüan: see Fu, senior monk
Tanrei Soden, d. 1701
Tao-hsin, Fourth Patriarch (Dōshin) 580–651
Tao-wu Yüan-chih (Dōgo Enchi) 769–835
Te-shan Hsüan-chien (Tokusan Senken) 780–865
Tenkei Denson, 1648–1735
Tettō Gikō, 1295–1369
T'ien-mu Liao-i (Tenmoku Ryōkai) n.d.
Tokuhō Zenketsu, 1419–1506
Tōrei Enji, 1721–1792
Tou-shuai Ts'ung-yüeh (Tosotsu Jūetsu) 1044–1091
T'ou-tzu Ta-tung (Tōsu Daidō) 819–914
Tōyō Eichō, 1428–1504
Ts'ao-shan Pen-chi (Sōzan Honjaku) 840–901
Ts'ui-wei Wu-hsüeh (Suibi Mugaku) n.d.
Ts'ui-yen K'e-hsin (Suigan Kashin) d. 1064
Ts'ui-yen Shou-chih (Suigan Shushi) n.d.
Tu-chan Hsing-ying (Dokutan Shōkei) 1628–1706
Tuan-ya Liao-i (Dangai Ryōgi) 1263–1334
Tung-shan: see Tung-shan Liang-chieh
Tung-shan Liang-chieh (Tōzan Ryōkai) 807–869
Tung-shan Hsiao-ts'ung (Tōzan Gyōsō) n.d.
Tung-shan Shou-ch'u (Tōzan Shusho) 910–990
Tung-ssu Ju-hui (Tōji Nyoe) 758–823
Tzu-hu Li-tsung (Shiko Rishō) 800–880
Tz'u-ming Ch'u-yüan (Jimyō Soen) 986–1039

Wan-an Tao-yen (Mannan Dōgan) 1094–1164
Wei, head monk (Ishō) n.d.
Wei-sheng Hsin-chüeh (Ishō Shinkaku) n.d.
Wen-chu Ying-hsin (Monju Ōshin) n.d.

Wu-chin, Layman (Mujin Kōji) 1043–1121
Wu-chun Shih-fan (Bushun Shihan) 1177–1249
Wu-hsüeh Tsu-yüan (Mugaku Sōgen) 1226–1286
Wu-ming Hui-ching (Mumyō Ekyō) 1548–1618
Wu-tsu Fa-yen (Goso Hōen) 1024–1104
Wu-tsu Shih-chieh (Goso Shikai) n.d.

Yang-ch'i Fang-hui (Yōgi Hōe) 992–1049
Yen-t'ou Ch'üan-huo (Gantō Zenkatsu) 828–887
Ying-an T'an-hua (Ō'an Donge) 1103–1163
Yüan-chien Fa-yüan (Enkan Hōen): see Fu-shan Yüan-chien
Yüan-hsien Yung-chiao (Genken Yōkaku) 1578–1657
Yüan-wu K'o-ch'in (Engo Kokugon) 1063–1135
Yün-an P'u-yen (Un'an Fugan) 1156–1226
Yün-ch'i Chu-hung (Unsei Shukō) 1535–1615
Yün-chü Tao-ying (Ungo Dōyō) d. 902
Yün-feng Wen-yüeh (Umpō Bun'etsu) 998–1062
Yün-men Wen-yen (Ummon Bun'en) 862–949
Yung-chia Hsüan-chüeh (Yōka Genkaku) 675–713
Yung-chiao: see Yüan-hsien Yung-chiao
Yung-ming Yen-shou (Yōmei Enju) 904–975

List of Texts

Admonitory Instructions for Buddhist Monks (Tsu-men ching-hsun; Shimon-keikun)

Amida Sutra (A-mi-t'o ching; Amida-kyō)

Amida Sutra, Commentary on the (A-mi-t'o ching su-ch'ao)

Annals of the Lineage of the Buddha-patriarchs (Fo-tsu t'ung-chi; Busso-tōki)

Biographies of Eminent Priests of the Great Ming (Ta-ming kao-seng chuan; Daimin kōsō-den)

Biographies of Eminent Priests, second series (Hsü Kao-seng chuan; Zoku kōsō-den)

Biographies of Monks of the Zen Groves (Ch'an-lin seng-pao chuan; Zenrin sōbō-den)

Blue Cliff Record (Pi-yen-lu; Hekigan-roku)

Bodhidharma's Six Gates (Shōshitsu rokumon)

Ch'an-yü nei-chi (Zen records of Yung-chiao; Zen'yō naishū)

Continuation of the Records of the Lamp (Hsü Ch'uan-teng lu; Zoku Dentō-roku)

Dharma Teachings of Fo-yen (Fo-yen ho-shang p'u-shuo; Butsugen oshō fusetsu)

Diamond Sutra (Chin-kang ching; Kongo-kyō)

Drop of Seawater for the Platform Sutra, A (Rokusodankyō kaisui-itteki)

Entering the Mud, Entering the Water (Wadei-gasui)

Essentials of the Mind Transmission (Ch'uan-hsin fa-yao; Denshin hōyō)

Essay on the Dharma Pulse, The (Hsüeh-mo lun; Ketsumyaku-ron)

Essay on the Nature of Awakening, The (Wu-hsing lun; Goshō-ron)

Essentials for Rebirth, The (Ōjō-yōshū)

Essentials of Successive Records of the Lamp (Lien-teng hui-yao; Rentō-eyō)

Everyday Sayings and Doings of Daitō Kokushi (Daitō Kokushi gyōjō)

Five Lamps, A Compendium of the (Wu-teng yüan-yao; Gotō-egen)

Flower Garland Sutra, The (Avatamsaka-sutra; Hua-yen ching; Kegon-kyō)

Flower Garland Sutra, Commentary on the (Hua-yen Ho-lun; Kegon-gōron)

Gateless Barrier, The (Wu-men kuan; Mumonkan)

Great Events in the Zen Groves (Ts'ung-lin sheng-shih; Sōrin-seiji)

Han-shan, Poems of (Han-shan shih; Kanzan-shi)

Hsüeh-tou's Hundred Koans with Verse Comments (Hsueh-tou po-tse sung-ku; Setchō hyakusoku juko)

Idle Talk on a Night Boat (Yasen-kanna)

Kokuyaku zenshū sōshō (A collection of Zen texts in Japanese translation)

Larger Sutra of Boundless Life (Sukhavati-vyūha; Wu-liang-shou ching; Daimur-yōju-kyō)

Lotus Sutra (Fa-hua ching; Hoke-kyō)

Meditation Sutra (Kuan wu-liang-shou ching; Kanmuryōju-kyō)

Model Teachings of the House of Zen (Sŏn-ga kyui-gam; Zenke-kikan)

Mountain Hermitage Miscellany (Shan-an tsa-lu; Sannan zatsuroku)

Nirvana Sutra (Nieh-p'an ching; Nehan-gyō)

Praise of the Five Houses (Wu-chia cheng-tsung tsan; Goke shōjū-san)

Platform Sutra (Liu-tsu t'an ching; Rokuso-dankyō)

Platform Sutra, Commentary on the (Rokusodankyō kōkan)

Precious Lessons of the Zen School (Ch'an-men pao-hsun; Zenmon hōkun)

Precious Mirror for Men and Gods (Jen-t'ien pao-chien; Ninden hōkan)

Records from the Groves of Zen (Lin-kuan lu; Rinkan-roku)

Records of Daiō (Daiō goroku)

Records of Daitō (Daiō goroku)

Records of Hsü-t'ang (Hsü-t'ang yü-lu; Kidō goroku)

Records of Kao-feng (Kao-feng yü-lu; Kōhō goroku)

Records of Lin-chi (Lin-chi yü-lu; Rinzai goroku)

Records of the Lamp of the Ching-te Era (Ching-te ch'uan-teng lu; Keitoku dentō-roku)

Records of the Lamp of the Empō Era (Empō dentō-roku)

Records of the Mirror Source (Tsung-ching lu; Sugyō-roku)

Records of Wu-tsu (Wu-tsu yü-lu; Goso goroku)

Rustic Records from Lo-hu (Lo-hu yeh-lu; Ragoyaroku)

Shurangama Sutra (Leng-yen ching; Ryōgon-kyō)

Shurangama Sutra, Commentary on the, (Leng-yen ching su-chieh meng-ch'ao; Ryōgon-kyō sokai mōshō)

Sokkō-roku kaien-fusetsu

Sokkō-roku kaien-fusetsu, Snake Legs for the (Sokkō-roku kaien-fusetsu dasoku)

Song on Realizing the Way (Cheng-tao ke; Shōdō-ka)

Sutra of Forty-two Sections (Ssu-shih-erh-chang ching; Shijūnishō-kyō)

Sutra of the Bequeathed Teaching (I-chiao ching; Yuikyō-kyō)

Sutra of Perfect Enlightenment (Yüan-chüeh ching; Engaku-kyō)

Sutra of Seven Women (Chi-yü ching; Shichinyo-kyō)

Sutra of the Victorious Kings of Golden Light (Suvarnaprabha-sottoma; Chin-kuang-ming tsui-sheng-wang ching; Konkōmyō saishōō-kyō)

Ta-hui's Arsenal (Ta-hui wu-k'u; Daie buko)

Ta-hui's Letters (Ta-hui shu; Dai-sho)

Treatise of the Precious Treasury (Pao-tsang lun; Hōzō-ron)

Wan-an's Words of Instruction (Wan-an ho-shang fa-yu; Mannan oshō hōgo)

Words from Dreamland (Kaian-kokugo)

Wild Ivy (Itsumadegusa)

NOTES

LICKING UP HSI-KENG'S FOX SLOBBER

1. Yüan-wu's lectures, *Hsüeh-tou's Hundred Koans with Verse Comments,* grew into *The Blue Cliff Record,* regarded as the most important single work of Rinzai Zen literature.

2. Ta-p'ing Hui-ch'in was, like Yüan-wu, a Dharma heir of Wu-tsu Fa-yen. Ta-p'ing's letter is found in a compilation titled *Admonitory Instructions for Buddhist Monks,* first published in the Yüan dynasty (1280–1368).

3. Fox slobber (*koen*) is a metaphor for a lethal poison; it can work miraculous cures by purging students of their mental illnesses and leading them to true enlightenment. Hakuin wrote, "Hsi-keng spewed up poisonous slobberings of word, thought, and deed and left them behind to await a future descendant who would be able to use them to turn his back on the master's (Hsi-keng's) teaching." Hsi-keng served as abbot at ten different temples during his career. The main body of his religious teaching, *The Records of Hsü-t'ang,* is divided into ten sections, with one section devoted to the teachings he gave at each of the ten temples.

4. Fei Lien and Wu Lai: evil ministers under King Chou.

5. A devil king who attempts to destroy all that is good.

6. An allusion to a story found in *Ta-hui's Arsenal,* ch. 2, a collection of Zen anecdotes compiled by the Sung priest Ta-hui Tsung-kao:

> Attendant P'ing served Zen master Ming-an for many years. Although he trained hard and was able to grasp the essentials of Ming-an's Zen, he was jealous of his fellow monks and attempted at every opportunity to discredit them. For this reason, Ming-an did not sanction him as his successor, despite his seniority. He told his other disciples that P'ing would meet with a violent death, which would occur, he said, holding up three fingers, "at a place like this." However, after Ming-an's death, Ping succeeded in becoming the master of the temple. He declared that the geomantic situation of Ming-an's memorial tower was unfavorable, and ordered it burned. As the fire consumed the tower, it collapsed and fell open, revealing Ming-an's corpse. To everyone's astonishment, it was unscathed by the flames and

still fresh as life. P'ing took up a hoe, split open Ming-an's skull, took out the brain, doused it with oil, and threw it back into the flames, where it was reduced to ashes. His fellow priests reported this to the civil authorities, who severely reprimanded P'ing and forced him to return to lay status. He wandered aimlessly around the country, trying without success to gain entrance to other Buddhist communities. One day, as he was walking near the intersection of three roads, he was attacked and devoured by a tiger, fulfilling his master's prophecy.

7. The priest whom Hakuin regarded as his master. The lineage is Gudō Tōshoku, 1579–1661; Shidō Mun'an, 1603–1676; Shōju Etan, 1642–1721; Hakuin.

8. A monk asked Chao-chou: "Does a dog have buddha-nature?" Chao-chou said: "Mu." See *The Gateless Barrier,* case 1, translated by Robert Aitken (San Francisco: North Point Press, 1991), p. 7. Initially, Hakuin gave students this as a first koan; later, in his sixties, he began to use "the sound of the single hand."

9. The phrase "one man or half a man" (*ikkō hankō*) emphasizes the difficulty, yet the absolute necessity, for a Zen master to find an heir to carry on his transmission, half a person being better than none at all.

10. In folk belief, people who trim their fingernails at night will not be at their parents' bedsides when they die. According to Hakuin, it was a favorite saying of Shōju's. Here it appears to caution against relaxing one's religious efforts.

THE POISONOUS LEAVINGS OF PAST MASTERS

1. This dialogue, from *Essentials of Successive Records of the Lamps,* ch. 33, is classed as a *nantō* ("hard-to-pass") koan in Hakuin Zen.

2. A teacher is said to lose his eyebrows for false or overly explicit preaching.

3. Reference to the koan Po-chang's Fox. *Gateless Barrier,* case 2, p. 19.

4. Hsü-t'ang Chih-yü, *Records of Hsü-t'ang,* ch. 4.

5. The twenty-eight Indian patriarchs in the Zen transmission from Shakyamuni to Bodhidharma, and the six Chinese patriarchs beginning with Bodhidharma and ending with Hui-neng.

6. An allusion to the teaching style of Hsüeh-feng I-ts'un, 822–908, a T'ang monk who traveled from temple to temple carrying a calabash dipper.

7. *The Essay on the Dharma Pulse,* traditionally ascribed to Bodhidharma, is included in a Japanese collection titled *Bodhidharma's Six Gates.*

8. Ch'ang-tsung Chao-chüeh is severely criticized in Ta-hui's writings as a propagator of "do-nothing" (*buji*) Zen.

9. Ta-hui was an outspoken opponent of the quietistic type of Zen that Hakuin also attacks. This entire section, thirteen paragraphs in all, beginning above with the words "Zen master Ch'ang-tsung Chao-chüeh . . ." is taken from *Ta-hui's Arsenal.*

10. These questions, known as "Huang-lung's Three Barriers," were devised by Hsin-ching's teacher, Huang-lung Hui-nan.

11. The eighth, or Alaya, consciousness is regarded as the source of human consciousness and all existence. When practicers penetrate to it they are considered to have finally succeeded in overcoming evil passions, but if they cling to it, it becomes another cause trapping them within birth and death. Hakuin exhorts students to "smash open the dark cave of the eighth consciousness" so that "the precious light of the Great Perfect Mirror Wisdom can shine forth."

12. In *The Sutra of Seven Women* [Taisho 14], Indra and the women visit the Buddha Kashyapa. Hakuin's account is based on that in *The Five Lamps,* ch. 1.

13. The four necessities are food, clothing, medicine, and shelter. The seven rare treasures are gold, silver, lapis lazuli, moonstone, agate, ruby, carnelian.

14. Cf. *The Zen Teachings of Master Lin-chi,* translated by Burton Watson (Shambhala, 1993), pp. 76, 127.

15. The ingredients are all lethal.

16. Nan-yüeh, seeing his student Ma-tsu practicing zazen, took a tile and began polishing it. When Ma-tsu asked him what he was doing, he replied that he was making a mirror. Ma-tsu told him that is was impossible to make a mirror from a tile. Nan-yüeh first replied, "And how do you expect to become a buddha by doing zazen?" Then he spoke the words Hakuin quotes here.

AUTHENTIC ZEN

1. In a lengthy section beginning here Hakuin cites a long chronological line of Indian, Chinese, and Japanese teachers (starting with Shakyamuni and ending with fifteenth-century Japanese priests of the Myōshin-ji Temple) whom he singles out for praise as authentic transmitters of the true Zen traditions.

2. According to Zen tradition, Shakyamuni's enlightenment occurred when he looked up and saw the morning star. Hakuin calls it a "bad star" (*akusei*), probably in the same sense as "poison drum" or "poison words," to emphasize the power it has to destroy illusion and lead to final enlightenment.

3. That is, living beings that are womb-born, egg-born, water-born, and born by metamorphosis.

4. The "four struts" (the characters also mean "four pillars") allude to the Four Noble Truths: pain or suffering, its cause, its ending, and the way thereto. The "twelve elegant tones" is the twelve-link chain of dependent origination: ignorance, actions produced by ignorance, emergence of consciousness, mental activity, the five senses and mind, sensory contact, perception, craving, attachment, existence, birth, old age and death.

   The "one vehicle" refers to the Mahayana teaching preached in *The Lotus Sutra.*

   The "final song" is *The Sutra of the Bequeathed Teaching,* which the Buddha is said to have preached before entering nirvana.

5. The first transmission of the Zen Dharma is said to have occurred when Shakyamuni held up a flower during a sermon, baffling everyone present except Kashyapa, "Great Turtle," who broke into a smile.

   The "instruments" are the twenty-eight Indian patriarchs from Shakyamuni to Bodhidharma.

   The "blue-eyed virtuoso" is Bodhidharma, who is described in Zen history as a prince from southern India; he refuted six celebrated religious teachers before he went to China. *Records of the Lamp, Empō Era* ch. 3.

   The Flower Garland Sutra speaks of music from a lute strung with lion gut muting all other instruments.

   The number eight alludes to eight transmissions from Bodhidharma to Ma-tsu Tao-i.

6. An allusion to the story of Bodhidharma transmitting his Dharma to his four disciples. After summoning them and hearing each express his attainment, Bodhidharma said to one, "You have my skin"; to another, "You have my flesh"; to a third, "You have my bones"; and to Hui-k'o, who became his successor, he said, "You have my marrow." According to legend, Bodhidharma was buried at Bear's Ears Mountain (Hsiung-erh shan).

7. The "old nag" is Ma-tsu (the name is literally "Horse Patriarch"), an heir of Nan-yüeh Huai-jang seven generations after Bodhidharma. Hui-neng, the Sixth Chinese Patriarch, told Nan-yüeh that the Indian patriarch Prajnatara had predicted that Nan-yüeh would produce a spirited young horse who would trample the world into dust. *Five Lamps,* ch. 3.

8. Yen-t'ou Ch'üan-huo taught people while working as a ferryman at the Ta-i Ford after he had been forced to return to lay status during a government suppression of Buddhism.

9. "Elephant Bones" (Hsiang-ku) was a name used for Mount Hsüeh-feng in present Fukien province; here it refers to Hsüeh-feng I-ts'un, who resided there.

   "Mount Lo" is master Lo-shan Tao-hsien; "Mount Su" is Su-shan Kuang-jen. "Yellow bell" and "great harmony" are names of two primary tones on the Chinese musical scale; they are used figuratively to indicate matters of elemental significance.

10. Kuang-t'ai yüan was the name of Yün-men's temple on Mount Yün-men in Kuang-nan (modern Kwangtung). The "eighty bodies" presumably refers to his Dharma heirs, and "countless others" to those who studied with him (he was said to have had over a thousand students) without receiving his formal certification.

11. Tung-shan Hsiao-ts'ung and Hsüeh-tou Ch'ung-hsien (co-author of *The Blue Cliff Record*), both of the Yün-men line.

12. The "iron lion" is Fen-yang Shan-chao, the teacher of Tz'u-ming Ch'u-yüan. The "straw dog" refers to Tzu-hu Li-tsung. Tzu-hu told people, "There's a dog around here with the head and the heart and the feet of a man." When people asked him about it, he went "Woof! Woof!"

13. Wu-tsu Fa-yen was born to the Teng family of Pa-hsi in Mien-chou, modern Szechwan. He practiced under Po-yün Shou-tuan (Po-yün means "white cloud"), eventually succeeding him. He lived for a time at Broken-head Peak (P'o-t'ou shan) at Mount Huang-mei. He spent his later years at Tung-shan (Eastern Mountain), in modern Hupeh.

    The "three buddhas" are Wu-tsu Fa-yen's disciples Fo-yen T'uan-yü, Fo-chien Hui-ch'in, and Zen master Fo-kuo (the honorary title of Yüan-wu K'o-ch'in), whose names begin with the character for "buddha."

    The "quiet man" is Ta-sui Nan-t'ung, another of Wu-tsu's disciples, whose honorary title, Yüan-ching, contains the character for "quiet."

14. Ta-hui Tsung-kao lived for a period at Heng-yang, in modern Hunan. Fo-chien is the honorary title of Wu-chun Shih-fan.

    The words *Dragon Pool* (Lung-yüan) were inscribed on a plaque in Fo-chien's chambers at his temple on Mount Ching.

    "Tiger Hill" (Hu-ch'iu) is Hu-ch'iu Shao-lung. "Yellow Dragon" (Huang-lung) is Huang-lung Hui-nan.

15. Ying-an T'an-hua was a Dharma heir of Hu-ch'iu Shao-lung; Mi-an, an heir of Ying-an; Sung-yüan Ch'ung-yüeh, an heir of Mi-an; and Yün-an P'u-yen, an heir of Sung-yüan.

16. Hsi-keng (Hsü-t'ang Chih-yü) was a native of Ssu-ming in present-day Chekiang province and received the transmission from Yün-an P'u-yen. He achieved enlightenment while working on the koan Su-shan's Memorial Tower, in which Su-shan says, "On Ta-yü Peak is an old buddha who emits dazzling shafts of light" (the full text of the koan is given in Isshu Miura and Ruth F. Sasaki's *Zen Koan* (New York: Harcourt, Brace and World, 1968), p. 60. Hsü-t'ang served at ten different temples during his career.

17. This is based on words in a prophecy that Bodhidharma's teacher Prajna-

tara made when Bodhidharma was about to leave India for China. The golden cock was startled to learn that now Daiō was taking the Dharma transmission to Japan; the jade tortoise was sad because he was not there to carry Daiō over the seas on this important mission. See Tokiwa Gishin, *Hakuin* (Tokyo, Chūokōron-sha, 1988), p. 67.

18. "Recumbent Mountain" translates Ōgaku-zan Sōfuku-ji, the "mountain name" of the Kyūshū Temple considered to be the first Rinzai Zen temple established in Japan. It was founded by Daiō Kokushi on his return after studying with Hsü-t'ang Chih-yü in China. In time, Daiō's line became the main branch of the Japanese Rinzai school.

"Purple Fields" (Murasakino) refers to the Daitoku-ji Temple, founded by Daiō's heir Daitō, and located in the Murasakino district of Kyoto.

"Deer darting by" alludes to the teaching style of the Chinese priest Wu-hsüeh Tsu-yüan. Wu-hsüeh was invited to Japan by Shogun Hōjō Tokimune, who built the Engaku-ji Temple for him in Kamakura; at the opening ceremony a herd of deer ran through the temple precincts. It was taken as an auspicious sign, and the temple was given the "mountain name" Zuiroku-zan ("Auspicious Deer Mountain"). See *Records of the Lamp of the Empō Era.* ch. 2.

The "bright pearl" refers to the Shinju-an ("Pearl Hermitage") subtemple of Daitoku-ji, and by extension to its founder Ikkyū Sōjun.

19. "Flower Fields" (Hanazono) refers to the Myōshin-ji Temple in Kyoto, which was established by Emperor Hanazono for Kanzan Egen, one of Daitō Kokushi's disciples.

The "eight sounds" refers to eight kinds of musical instruments: bell, drum, wind, etc.

The "four pillars" are the four disciples of Sekkō Sōshin, the priest credited with restoring Myōshin-ji after its destruction in the Ōnin War (1467). These four disciples—Keisen Sōryū (1425–1500), Gokei Sōton (1416–1500), Tokuhō Zenketsu (1419–1506), and Tōyō Eichō (1428–1504)—founded the four main branches of the Myōshin-ji school. Hakuin was affiliated to the branch founded by Tōyō Eichō.

20. None of these three priests has any known connection with the Pure Land teaching. Hakuin's reason for naming them here is unclear.

21. This reference is based on a verse by Yüan-wu K'o-ch'in: "Worship the Sixth Patriarch, an authentic old buddha who manifested himself in the human world as a 'good teacher' for eighty lifetimes in order to help others." Tōrei Enji's *Snake Legs for the Kaien-fusetsu,* p. 21 verso.

22. *Sutra of Meditation on the Buddha of Boundless Life* is one of the principal texts of the Pure Land tradition.

23. The identification of Rushana Buddha (signifying Illuminating) with the

Sambhoga-kaya, distinguishing him from Birushana (Vairochana, the central Buddha of *The Flower Garland Sutra*), who is the Dharma-kaya, and from Shakyamuni (the Illuminated, or Enlightened One), the Nirmana-kaya, is a doctrine of the T'ien-t'ai school.

24. From *The Essay on the Nature of Enlightenment*.

25. From *The Essentials of the Mind Transmission*.

26. Quoted from the sutra's second chapter ("Distinguishing the Three Buddha-bodies").

27. The six "dusts" (Sanskrit, *guna*), or objects of perception (corresponding to the six sense organs): color and form, odor, taste, sound, tactile objects, and mental objects.

28. According to *The Meditation Sutra,* to be assured of rebirth in the Pure Land, a practicer of the *nembutsu* must attain the "triple mind" (*sanshin*), the mind of perfect sincerity, the mind that deeply desires rebirth, and the mind that vows to turn its merits to benefit others; and the "fourfold practice" (*shishu*), to practice *nembutsu alone,* constantly, with reverence, and for an entire lifetime.

29. A saying found in Yung-ming Yen-shou's *Records of the Mirror Source*. Yen-shou favored the combining of Zen and Pure Land practices. Wings would make a tiger even more formidable.

30. Old Clam (Rō-rakō) was a pseudonym used by the Sōtō priest Tenkei Denson, 1648–1735. He served as abbot at several temples in the Naniwa (Ōsaka) area. Shellfish were said to sleep for a thousand years; buddhas appear only rarely in the world.

31. This quotation is found in Tenkei's commentary on *The Platform Sutra, A Drop of Sea Water for the Platform Sutra,* ch. 3. *Zengaku Taikei,* soshibu 1 (Tokyo, 1911), p. 68.

32. Mineo Daikyū attributes this to Tenkei. *Kaienfusetsu-kōwa* (Chūobukkyō-sha, Tokyo, 1934) p. 243.

33. An annotation Hakuin inscribed in his copy of the *Kaien-fusetsu* identifies this person as a "priest of the Saigan-ji Temple, a Jōdo (Pure Land) temple in the village of Negoya, near the Hara post-station" (where Hakuin's own temple, Shōin-ji, was located).

34. Tu-chan Hsing-ying, a Chinese priest of the Ōbaku Zen sect. The Shozan (Hatsuyama) Hōrin-ji is a temple he founded in present Shizuoka prefecture.

35. The Sixth Patriarch is answering a questioner who wants to know if invoking the name of Amida Buddha will enable the caller to be born in Amida Buddha's Pure Land in the West. The ten evil acts are killing, stealing, adultery, lying, duplicity of speech, coarse language, idle talk,

greed, anger, and false views. The eight false acts are ones that run counter to the eightfold holy path, which is right views, thoughts, speech, acts, living, effort, mindfulness, and meditation.

36. Although frequently attacked in Hakuin's writings, Yün-ch'i Chu-hung is regarded in China as one of the most eminent priests of the Ming period. His commentary on *The Amida Sutra* (*A-mi-t'o ching su-ch'ao*) is one of his most important works.

37. In two of the three principal Pure Land sutras, *The Amida Sutra* and *The Larger Sutra of Boundless Life,* Amida Buddha's Pure Land is said to lie to the west, distant by millions upon millions of buddha-lands. The third, *The Meditation Sutra,* contains the statement that the Pure Land is "not far from here."

38. This is probably Hakuin himself.

39. One of the vows made by Amida Buddha as given in *The Larger Sutra of Boundless Life* states that at the moment of death Amida Buddha will appear before all those who have heard his name and meditated upon him and conduct them to his Pure Land.

40. Hui-neng received the Zen transmission from the Fifth Patriarch Hung-jen at the latter's temple on Mount Huang-mei, in modern Hupeh.

41. The priest Ch'ang-sha Ching-ts'en declared that "the world in all ten directions is the eye of the Zen monk." A monk asked, "What is the eye of the Zen monk?" "Nothing ever leaves it," said the master. *Records of the Lamp,* ch. 10.

42. The Shining Land of Lapis Lazuli in the East is the buddha-land of Yakushi, the Healing Buddha (Bhaishajyaguru). The Immaculate Land of Purity in the South is a buddha-land mentioned in *The Lotus Sutra.*

43. *The Meditation Sutra* divides aspirants for birth in the Pure Land into nine ranks according to their capacities, beginning with those of the "highest rank of the highest birth."

44. Han-tan, a poor scholar on his way to take the imperial examinations, stopped and took a nap. He dreamed he passed the examinations with flying colors and had an illustrious career. When he woke up, he realized that life is an empty dream, and returned home.

45. The Sixth Patriarch was said to be a poor, unlettered peasant from the backward, southern part of the country.

46. The author of the commentary is given as Eikijun. It was first published in Kyoto in 1697.

47. Legendary founder of an ancient Chinese dynasty.

48. Nan-hai Tsung-pao, a Zen priest of the Yüan dynasty, edited a text of *The*

Platform Sutra that was published in 1291. The passage quoted here appears in his postface to that edition.

49. Queen Vaidehi was the wife of Bimbisara, king of Magadha. When her son imprisoned her, the Buddha, out of compassion, appeared in answer to her prayers and taught her how to attain the Pure Land of Amida Buddha. The story forms the basis of *The Meditation Sutra.*

50. The commentary is by Li Tsung-hsüan of the T'ang dynasty. In it, Li enumerates six "vehicles," corresponding to the capabilities of sentient beings, by which they can attain "the mind of the Mahayana." The first two lead to rebirth in the Pure Land, while the sixth and highest vehicle brings instantaneous attainment of buddhahood.

51. One of Chu-hung's titles.

52. The cave near Rajagrha where the first collection of Buddhist sutras is said to have been compiled.

53. Huang Ti, who in 212 BCE ordered the burning of the Chinese classics.

54. Imperial proscriptions of Buddhism were decreed during the Northern Wei (444–446), the Northern Chou (574–577), and the T'ang dynasty (843–845).

55. In this passage Hakuin paraphrases from Bassui Tokushō's Japanese work *Entering the Mud, Entering the Water (Wadeigasui).*

56. This paragraph is a loose paraphrase from several works, chiefly *The Essay on the Dharma Pulse,* in *Bodhidharma's Six Gates.*

THE DIFFICULTY OF REPAYING THE DEBT TO THE BUDDHAS AND THE PATRIARCHS

1. Hakuin continues in these first paragraphs to paraphrase freely from the writings of Bodhidharma (cf. preceding section, fn. 56).

2. The quotation is found in Kao-feng's Zen records. Hakuin takes it from *Model Teachings of the House of Zen.*

3. The parable of the priceless jewel, representing the Buddha's most profound teaching, is from *The Lotus Sutra.*

4. The Dragon Gates (Lung-men) is a section of the Yellow River where the current flows with tremendous force through a narrow gorge. It is said to have been opened by Emperor Yü (the Great Yü). Carp who fight their way upstream past this "barrier" are said to transform into dragons.

5. The allusion is to a stork that did not perform when its owner's boasts brought friends to see it.

6. This is from the *Leng-yen ching su-chieh meng-ch'ao,* compiled by Ch'ia ch'ien-i at the end of the Ming dynasty.

7. From the "Song on Realizing the Way" by Yung-chia Hsüan-chüeh: "See the man who has cut himself free from the way of practice, who is taking it easy with nothing to do, / Neither brushing illusion away nor seeking the truth of enlightenment."

8. The phrase "reverting to tranquillity, living within it" (*tannyū gōtan*), from the *Shurangama Sutra,* describes the attainment of a state of tranquillity that, because attachment remains, is still incomplete. *Ta-hui's Letters.* Araki Kengo, *Daie-sho* (Chikuma-shobō, Tokyo, 1969), p. 27.

9. *Ta-hui's Letters,* ibid., p. 206.

10. Of the eight consciousnesses posited by the Yogachara school, the eighth, Alaya or storehouse consciousness, located below the realm of conscious awareness, is the deepest ground of the self and the source of the first seven consciousnesses, which are produced from "seeds" stored within it. As the condition of illusion in those not fully awakened, it is regarded as that which undergoes birth and death. Hakuin refers to students who have attained a state of tranquillity and attach to it in the belief it is ultimate, describing them as "nesting" within the "dark cave of the eighth consciousness." When this "dark cave" is completely "overturned," or "inverted," it transforms into the so-called Great Perfect Mirror Wisdom (*Daienkyōchi*), which is free of all defiling illusion and reflects things as they truly are. The "Fivefold Eye" (*Go-gen*) enables vision and insight of every kind: of the human eye, Deva eye, wisdom eye, Dharma eye, and buddha eye.

11. According to tradition, Shakyamuni preached *The Flower Garland Sutra,* containing the essence of his attainment, immediately after his enlightenment. Upon finding it was beyond the ability of ordinary people to comprehend, he resolved to refrain from further teaching, but he later reconsidered and accommodated his preaching to make it more accessible. In *The Blue Cliff Record* (Case 6), Yüan-wu K'o-ch'in describes the Buddha divesting himself of a sublime robe covered with precious (Dharma) gems far beyond the ability of ordinary mortals to appreciate, and donning common garments to preach within the defiled world.

12. The reference is to the twenty-four Zen priests, fourteen Chinese and ten Japanese, regarded as having introduced separate teaching lines into Japan during this 150-year period. The Divine Mulberry and Dragonfly Provinces are poetical references to Japan.

13. This statement is similar to the words the Sixth Patriarch spoke when he transmitted his Dharma to his disciple Nan-yüeh Huai-jang.

14. Here Hakuin has translated into Chinese, and paraphrased, a Japanese *waka* poem attributed to Daitō Kokushi.

15. Ta-hui Tsung-kao (a disciple of Yüan-wu) identifies the book in question as the Zen records of Hsin-ching K'o-wen. See Tokiwa, *Hakuin,* p. 285.

16. One day, speaking to his assembly, Yüan-wu said, "When a monk asked Yün-men, 'Where do all the buddhas come from?' Yün-men replied, 'The Eastern Mountain walks over the water.' But not me . . . I would say, 'A fragrant breeze comes of itself from the south, and in the palace pavilion a refreshing coolness stirs.' " *The Zen Koan,* pp. 163–64. At these words, Ta-hui, "his entire body running with sweat," suddenly attained enlightenment, and "distinctions of past, present, and future ceased to exist." *Five Lamps,* ch. 15.

17. Seeing that Ta-hui had become attached to his enlightenment, Yüan-wu appointed him as a special attendant, freeing him from all duties, so he was able to go to Yüan-wu's chambers for personal instruction three or four times daily. Each time, Yüan-wu would quote a Zen saying by T'ang master Ch'ang-ch'ing Ta-an: "Being and nonbeing is like a wisteria vine wrapped around a tree," and ask, "What does that mean?" Whatever Ta-hui said or did, Yüan-wu would immediately declare, "That's not it!" Six months later, at a total impasse, Ta-hui asked Yüan-wu, "When you were with your master Fa-yen, I understand you asked him that same question. What did he say?" At first Yüan-wu just laughed, but finally he told Ta-hui, "He said, 'No depiction could do justice to it.' Then I asked, 'What happens when the tree falls and the wisteria withers?' He said, 'The same thing happens.' " When Ta-hui heard those words, he was finally enlightened.

18. *Blue Cliff Record,* Case 25.

19. Nan-ch'üan P'u-yüan, living by himself in a small hut, was visited by a monk. Nan-ch'üan told the monk he had work to do up the mountain and asked him to bring some food to him at mealtime. When the monk didn't show up, Nan-ch'üan returned and found the cooking vessels smashed and the monk fast asleep. Thereupon he took a nap himself, and when he woke up, the monk was gone. In later years, Nan-ch'üan said, "Back when I was living by myself, I had a visit from a splendid monk. I've never seen him since."

Tokiwa suggests a possible connection between Wan-an Tao-yen's verse comment and the following story. A laywoman was studying with Ta-hui while Wan-an was head monk at Ta-hui's temple. Over Wan-an's objections, Ta-hui allowed the woman to stay in the monk's quarters, on the grounds that "she was no ordinary woman." Finally, at Ta-hui's insistence, Wan-an went to talk with her. She asked if he wished a worldly encounter or a spiritual one. He indicated the latter, but when he entered her room, he found her lying flat on her back, completely naked. "What kind of place is that? said Wan-an, pointing at her. "The place whence all the buddhas of the Three Worlds, all six Zen patriarchs, and all the venerable priests in the land have emerged," she replied. "Would you allow me to enter?" he asked. "It isn't a place donkeys and horses can go," she said. Wan-an was unable to reply. "The meeting is over," she said, turning her back to him. "Hakuin zenji *Sokkō-roku kaien-fusetsu* o yonde," *Annual Reports of Researches of Matsugaoka Bunko,* no. 4, 1990, pp. 105–7.

20.   1. What is the Way? A clear-eyed man falls into a well.

2. What is the blown-hair sword? Each branch on the coral holds up the moon.

3. A monk asked Pa-ling, "What is the school of Devadatta?" He replied, "Filling a silver bowl with snow." *Blue Cliff Record,* Case 13.

21.   This paragraph and the next two consist of three separate passages taken from different parts of *The Blue Cliff Record:* the first paragraph is from Yüan-wu's introductory statement in Case 77 (except for Hakuin's own comment, "What a pitiful sight!"); the second paragraph is from Case 77; the third paragraph is from Case 53.

22.   The story of Nan-ch'üan's death is a famous *nantō* ("difficult-to-pass") koan. When Nan-ch'üan was about to die, the head monk asked him where he would be a hundred years hence. "A water buffalo at the foot of the hill," he answered. "Do you mind if I follow you?" asked the monk. "If you do," replied Nan-ch'üan, "you must hold a stalk of grass in your mouth."

23.   When Hui-neng was nearing death, Shih-t'ou, then a novice monk, came and asked him where he should continue his study. Hui-neng answered, "Investigate thoroughly." Ch'ang-sha's reply, "Investigate him thoroughly," parallels Hui-neng's answer.

24.   "Relics" are tiny gemlike fragments, said to be of such hardness that they are virtually indestructible, that are found among the ashes of a person of exceptional virtue after the body has been cremated.

25.   The full quotation is: "Within heaven and earth, in the midst of the universe, there is here a precious jewel lying hidden inside a mountain of form." The *Treatise* was attributed to the Chinese scholar-monk Seng-chao, 374–414.

26.   The quotation is from *The Mountain Hermitage Miscellany,* a Ming dynasty collection of Zen anecdotes by Shu-chung Wu-yün, 1309–1386.

27.   From *Records from the Groves of Zen,* by Chüeh-fan Hui-hung.

28.   From *Precious Lessons of the Zen School,* ch. 2.

29.   A monk asked Ta-sui Fa-chen, "When the world-ending kalpa fire comes and everything is consumed in the conflagration, will 'this' too be destroyed?" "Yes, destroyed," replied Ta-sui. "Then does 'it' go along with the rest?" asked the monk. " 'It' goes along," replied Ta-sui. *Blue Cliff Record,* Case 29.

30.   This story appears in *Praise of the Five Schools,* ch. 4.

31. The Central Asian monk Seng-ch'ieh (628–710) lived in Ssu-chou (Chiang-su province), helping those in need and always carrying a willow branch in his hand. When people asked, "What is your name?" he answered, "My name is what." When they asked, "What land are you from?" he said, "I'm from what land." He became known as the Great Sage of Ssu-chou (Ssu-chou Ta-sheng), and was revered as an incarnation of the Bodhisattva Kannon.

32. Tokiwa interprets this differently. His Japanese translation reads, "A gentleman loves his wealth, but there is always a way to get it away from him." *Hakuin*, p. 140.

33. This saying is not found in *The Analects*.

34. The material in this passage comes from *Praise of the Five Schools*, ch. 2.

35. Kao-an Shan-wu was an heir of Fo-yen Ch'ing-yüan (see the previous two paragraphs) who, like Yüan-wu, belonged to the line of Wu-tsu Fa-yen.

36. East Mountain (Tung-shan) is another name for Mount Wu-tsu (Wu-tsu shan) where Fa-yen lived.

37. This is from *The Records of Hsi-keng* (Hsü-t'ang Chih-yü). Hsü-t'ang's words continue, "When it is true, neither gods nor demons can penetrate its reason. When it prospers, they are quickly jealous of its good fortune." *Kokuyaku zenshū sōsho* II, vol. 6, p. 369.

THE TRUE AND UNTRANSMITTABLE DHARMA

1. The following episode is based largely on an account found in the supplement to *The Biographies of Monks of the Zen Groves*.

2. Tung-shan Shou-ch'u went to study with Zen master Yün-men. Yün-men asked where he came from. "From the Ch'a crossing," he said. "Where were you for the summer retreat?" asked Yün-men. "Pao-tz'u-ssu Temple in Hunan," he replied. "When did you leave?" he asked. "On the twenty-fifth of the eighth month," he said. "I'm going to spare you the three beatings you've earned," said Yün-men. That night, Shou-ch'u went to Yün-men's chambers and asked what he had done to deserve a beating. "You worthless rice bag," said Yün-men. "Going off like that, west of the river, and south of the lake." With this, Shou-ch'u attained great enlightenment.

3. A monk on his way to Mount Wu-t'ai asked an old woman he met by the side of the road, "Which is the way to Wu-t'ai?" "Right straight ahead," she replied. As the monk was about to walk on, she said, "Another one fell for it." When master Chao-chou heard about this, he immediately went to the place himself and asked her, "Which way is it to Wu-t'ai?" "Right straight ahead," she replied. As he was about to walk on, she said,

"There goes another one." Chao-chou returned to the temple, told his monks what had happened, and said, "Today, I saw right through that old woman." From *The Five Lamps,* ch. 4.

4. At this point Hakuin breaks off the dialogue between Hsin-ching and Shang-lan and inserts a separate dialogue between Po-chang Huai-hai and his monks. This continues for five paragraphs, followed by a paragraph of comments by Hakuin; then the interrupted story is resumed.

5. When Lin-chi was studying with Huang-po, he asked him three times about the meaning of the Buddhadharma, and each time Huang-po struck him. Po-yün Shou-tuan's verse comment is: "With one blow, he demolishes the Yellow Crane Tower; / With one kick, he turns Parrot Island on its back. / When the spirit is there, fuel it with more spirit. / Where there is no elegance, there too is elegance." The first two lines are taken from a celebrated verse by the poet Ts'uei Hao.

6. Hakuin includes this koan, Po-yün's 'Not Yet There,' among the *nantō* koans.

7. A saying of Chao-chou.

8. Nan-yang Hui-chung was a disciple of the Sixth Patriarch who lived on Mount Po-ai in Nan-yang for forty years. He lectured before emperors Su-tsung and Tai-tsung, and received from the latter the honorary title "National Master." The koan Hui-chung's Seamless (Memorial) Tower is Case 18 in *The Blue Cliff Record.*

9. "A man of Ch'i lived with his wife and concubine. Whenever he went out, he returned full of food and drink, telling his inquiring wife and concubine that he had dined with men of wealth and consequence. But they were suspicious, since no people of distinction ever came to their house. One day, the wife followed him. He led her throughout the city, arriving at last at the graveyard at the outskirts of the city. There he began begging leftovers from the parties of people who were offering sacrifices to the dead. When the wife returned home, she said to the concubine, "We looked up to our husband in hopeful contemplation. We cast our lot with him for life; and now these are his ways!" *Mencius,* IV, 33. Adapted from Legge's translation.

10. This account of Tou-shuai's meeting with Ch'ing-su begins a long section that Hakuin splices together from accounts in a number of different works. His main source is *Rustic Records from Lo-hu* (ch. 2), a twelfth century collection of Zen anecdotes with comments by the compiler Shu-chung Wu-yün.

11. A saying of Le-p'u Yüan-an. *Records of the Lamp, Ching-te Era* ch. 16.

12. The appraisal of Chüeh-fan and Layman Wu-chin that appears in these

two paragraphs, though it is not mentioned in the text, is by Shu-chung Wu-yün, in *Rustic Records,* ch. 2.

13. The encounter between Po-chang and Ma-tsu forms Case 53 of *The Blue Cliff Record,* "Po-chang's Wild Ducks."

    The story of Lin-chi and Huang-po is found in the "pilgrimage" section of *The Records of Lin-chi.* The phrase "loses his country" appears in *The Blue Cliff Record,* Case 61: "If you set up even one mote of dust, the country flourishes. If you do not set up one mote of dust, the country perishes."

    Feng-hsüeh's meeting with Nan-yüan is given in Yüan-wu's commentary on Case 38 of *The Blue Cliff Record.*

    Once Hsüeh-feng and Yen-t'ou were snowed in together in a mountain temple. While Yen-t'ou slept, Hsüeh-feng devoted himself conscientiously to zazen. Hsüeh-feng complained about making no progress despite all his effort. Yen-t'ou suggested that he sleep too. Hsüeh-feng replied that he couldn't because his mind was still not at rest. Yen-t'ou gave a loud "Khat!" and Hsüeh-feng was enlightened. Cf. *Five Lamps,* ch. 7.

    Yün-men visited Mu-chou and repeatedly asked for his teaching, but Mu-chou just turned him away. Yün-men finally managed to slip inside Mu-chou's hermitage but was discovered by Mu-chou, who thereupon demanded that Yün-men say something. As Yün-men was about to speak, the master shoved him out of the room, slamming the door on him and breaking one of his legs. With that, Yün-men was enlightened. *Blue Cliff Record,* Case 6.

    Chih-kuan's story appears in the text; see p. 93.

    The first two years Tz'u-ming studied with Fen-yang, Fen-yang refused to allow him in his chambers, berated him whenever he saw him, and gave him only the most elementary teachings. When Tz'u-ming finally complained that he wasn't making any progress, Fen-yang began scolding him angrily. He raised his staff and drove Tz'u-ming backward. Tz'u-ming threw up his arms to ward off the blows, and as he did, Fen-yang suddenly covered Tz'u-ming's mouth with his hand. With that, Tz'u-ming was enlightened. *Five Lamps,* ch. 12.

    Ts'ui-yen K'e-hsin was an heir of Tz'u-ming. As a young monk with an inflated opinion of his attainment, he attended a summer retreat with an attendant named Shan. One day, the two monks were walking down a mountain path engaged in conversation. Shan picked up a broken tile, placed it on top of a large rock, and said, "If you can utter a 'turning phrase' right now, I'll know you really studied with Master Tz'u-ming." Ts'ui-yen couldn't make any response. *Five Lamps,* ch. 12.

    A high official named Chang came to Wu-tsu Fa-yen's temple to ask about Zen. Fa-yen said, "As a young man, did you ever read a love poem about a beautiful woman with the verse, 'She calls constantly for her servant Little Jade, but doesn't really need her; She calls because she wants her lover to hear her voice'? Those lines are very close to Zen." "I know the lines," said Chang. "Concentrate on them single-mindedly," said Fa-yen.

Fa-yen's disciple Yüan-wu, who had heard all this, later asked Fa-yen, "Do you think he understood that poem?" "He only got the part about the calling," said Fa-yen. When Yüan-wu asked what Chang had failed to understand, Fa-yen said, "What is the meaning of the First Patriarch's coming from the West? The Cypress Tree in the Garden. *See!!!*" With that, Yüan-wu experienced enlightenment. *Five Lamps,* ch. 19.

Ta-yüan's (senior monk Fu's) story appears in *Five Lamps,* ch. 7.

Ta-hui was enlightened upon hearing his teacher Yüan-wu say, "A fragrant breeze comes of itself from the south, and in the palace pavilion a refreshing coolness stirs." See above, p. 73.

14. A reference to Shakyamuni's enlightenment, said to have occurred when he looked up and saw the morning star.

15. A verse comment in *The Blue Cliff Record,* Case 20.

16. There is no "Year of the Ass"; hence, never.

17. Hsi-keng (Hsü-t'ang) attained enlightenment while working on the koan The Old Sail Not Yet Raised: A monk asked Yen-t'ou, "What about when the old sail is not yet raised?" "Little fish swallow big fish," he replied. "What about after it's raised?" the monk asked. Yen-t'ou answered, "A donkey eats grass in the garden out back." Hsü-t'ang went to the chambers of his teacher Yün-an P'u-yen to inform him of his breakthrough. The moment he entered the door, the master could tell he had penetrated the koan, but instead of asking him about it, he asked him about another koan, Nan-ch'üan Kills the Cat. Hsü-t'ang replied immediately, "There's nowhere on earth to put it." Yün-an smiled, confirming Hsü-t'ang's understanding. For about a half year after that, Hsü-t'ang's mind was still not at peace, and when he engaged others in dialogue, he did not feel free. He left Yün-an and worked for four years on Su-shan's Memorial Tower. One day he suddenly grasped "the point at which the old Buddha on Ta-yü Peak emits shafts of dazzling light" (a phrase that appears in that koan). From then on, he was perfectly free, and his great pride that had made him despise other students vanished. Now, when he looked at koans he had previously penetrated, his understanding of them was altogether different, and he realized clearly that it had nothing at all to do with words. *Records of Hsü-t'ang,* ch. 4. For the koan Su-shan's Memorial Tower, see *The Zen Koan,* p. 60.

18. Daitō Kokushi was founder of the Daitoku-ji Temple in Kyoto and the chief heir of Daiō Kokushi, who had attained enlightenment while studying in China under Hsü-t'ang. Hakuin quotes from the "turning words"

that Daitō used to teach his students: "In the morning our eyebrows meet. We brush shoulders in the evening. What am I like? The temple pillars come and go all day long. Why don't I move? If you can penetrate these turning phrases, the matter for which you have devoted yourselves to a life of practice is completed." *The Everyday Sayings and Doings of Daitō Kokushi.*

19. Kanzan Egen, the chief heir of Daitō Kokushi and the founder of Myōs-hin-ji in Kyoto. Chao-chou's Cypress Tree in the Garden is Case 37 in *The Gateless Barrier.*

20. These words appear in a verse Hsū-t'ang gave Nampo Jōmyō (later Daiō Kokushi) when the latter was about to return home to Japan (see the introduction): "He visited Zen teachers, practiced with great devotion; / Where the path came to an end, he kept on going [or, His search at an end, he returns to his homeland]; / Clearly, Jōmyō preaches together with old Hsū-t'ang; / My descendants will increase daily beyond the Eastern Sea." From *The Records of Daiō;* also *Records of the Lamp from the Empō Era,* ch. 3.

INDEX OF PROPER NOUNS

(Continued on next page)

The Tibetan Book of the Dead: The Great Liberation through Hearing in the Bardo. Translated with commentary by Francesca Fremantle & Chögyam Trungpa.

Vitality, Energy, Spirit: A Taoist Sourcebook. Translated & edited by Thomas Cleary.

Wen-tzu: Understanding the Mysteries, by Lao-tzu. Translated by Thomas Cleary.

Worldly Wisdom: Confucian Teachings of the Ming Dynasty. Translated & edited by J. C. Cleary.

Zen Dawn: Early Zen Texts from Tun Huang. Translated by J. C. Cleary.

Zen Essence: The Science of Freedom. Translated & edited by Thomas Cleary.

The Zen Teachings of Master Lin-chi. Translated by Burton Watson.